Series/Number 07-162

QUANTITATIVE NARRATIVE ANALYSIS

Roberto Franzosi

Emory University

[handwritten inscription: To Gardee with gratitude for her friendship and for the stories we shared]

⊛SAGE

Los Angeles | London | New Delhi
Singapore | Washington DC

For information:

SAGE Publications, Inc.
2455 Teller Road
Thousand Oaks,
 California 91320
E-mail: order@sagepub.com

SAGE Publications India Pvt. Ltd.
B 1/I 1 Mohan Cooperative
 Industrial Area
Mathura Road, New Delhi 110 044
India

SAGE Publications Ltd.
1 Oliver's Yard
55 City Road
London EC1Y 1SP
United Kingdom

SAGE Publications
 Asia-Pacific Pte. Ltd.
33 Pekin Street #02-01
Far East Square
Singapore 048763

Printed in the United States of America

Library of Congress Cataloging-in-Publication Data

Franzosi, Roberto.
Quantitative narrative analysis/Roberto Franzosi.
 p. cm.—(Quantitative applications in the social sciences; 162)
Includes bibliographical references and index.
ISBN 978-1-4129-2525-9 (pbk.)
 1. Social sciences—Research—Methodology. 2. Discourse analysis, Narrative.
3. Content analysis (Communication) I. Title.

H61.F639 2010
306.44—dc22   2009014357

This book is printed on acid-free paper.

09   10   11   12   13   10   9   8   7   6   5   4   3   2   1

Acquisitions Editor:	Vicki Knight
Associate Editor:	Lauren Habib
Editorial Assistant:	Ashley Dodd
Production Editor:	Brittany Bauhaus
Copy Editor:	QuADS Prepress (P) Ltd.
Typesetter:	C&M Digitals (P) Ltd.
Proofreader:	Caryne Brown
Indexer:	Rick Hurd
Cover Designer:	Candice Harman
Marketing Manager:	Stephanie Adams

CONTENTS

ABOUT THE AUTHOR

Roberto Franzosi is Professor of Sociology and Linguistics at Emory University. He earned a BA in Literature from the University of Genoa (Italy) and a PhD in Sociology from Johns Hopkins University. After a postdoctoral year at the University of Michigan, he taught at the University of Wisconsin-Madison, Oxford University (with a fellowship at Trinity College), and University of Reading. His main research interests have been in social protest (e.g., *The Puzzle of Strikes: Class and State Strategies in Postwar Italy*, 1994). He has had a long-standing interest in issues of language and measurement of meaning, with several articles published and two books, *From Words to Number: Narrative, Data, and Social Science* (2005), and *Content Analysis* (2008).

SERIES EDITOR'S INTRODUCTION

Quantitative social science analysis requires the input of numerical data, most of which come in two forms—data recording human behavior and data recording human attitudes. These data are often at the individual level, but sometimes they can be at an aggregate level, such as city, county, province, canton, state, and country. The majority of the volumes in the Quantitative Applications in the Social Sciences series deal with analysis of these types of data by a variety of methods and models, such as linear regression, covariance structure, quantile regression, logit, probit, and generalized linear models.

The data dealt with in this volume represent a different type, texts that record human events, experiences, expressions, and emotions, and can be subject to either qualitative/interpretative or quantitative analysis. Whereas storytelling and narratives are as old as the history of the human species, with their informal analysis almost as old, the quantitative analysis of narratives is a much more recent scientific endeavor. This book, authored by Roberto Franzosi, an international authority on quantitative narrative analysis, offers a thorough and careful treatment of the topic of the quantitative analysis of narrative or text data in an engaging prose.

A typical social scientist must have heard of, if not performed, content analysis. It is easy to confuse quantitative narrative analysis with content analysis. The two methods, while sharing the drive to quantify, differ fundamentally, as Franzosi clarifies in the opening chapter, in that the categories of the former are based on the linguistic properties of narratives and that the categories of the latter are driven by the researcher's theoretical or substantive interest. It is difficult to say which approach is more scientific—perhaps it is only fair to say that each has its own merits—but it is at least useful to note that the design of content analysis is more of a top-down type, whereas that of quantitative narrative analysis has more of a bottom-up nature. Quantitative narrative analysis allows the data to speak more, if I may characterize the approach from an observer's point of view.

Drawing on decades of experience in conducting research in and teaching quantitative narrative analysis, Franzosi takes us on a grand tour of the beautiful realm of words—words that may come from classic narrative studies or even sociological classics themselves—and demonstrates the power of quantitative narrative analysis, its basics and rules, and its applications in computer software. By the end of the journey, the reader has traveled from words to numbers and back to words, following the masterful guidance of the author. The provision of such guidance is of no small task; Franzosi worked long and hard on the book, offering the series a *unique* contribution that fills a void in the social scientist's methodological toolbox. His eloquent prose makes the methodological reading, too often boring and dry, not only bearable but actually enjoyable.

—*Tim F. Liao*
Series Editor

PREFACE

On May 25, 1961, U.S. President John F. Kennedy delivered a speech before a joint session of Congress with a bold challenge: "I believe that this nation should commit itself to achieving the goal, before this decade is out, of landing a man on the moon and returning him safely to the Earth." Many derided the goal as lunacy. But on June 20, 1969, televisions across the world beamed the image of Apollo 11 commander Neil Armstrong jumping up and down on the dusty lunar soil. In those 8 years, between 1961 and 1969, new technologies had to be developed (rockets, space suits, communication) and tested over several successive space missions (Mercury, Gemini, Apollo).

In 1982, while a postdoc at the Center for Research on Social Organization at the University of Michigan, directed by Charles Tilly, I had a far less ambitious dream of my own: to carry out a project on the rise of Italian fascism (1919–1922) based on the statistical analysis of words taken from newspaper articles of the period. As for Kennedy, the realization of my dream required the development of many methodological and theoretical new tools (and several research grants). And like Kennedy, for years, I navigated without knowing (1) whether I would eventually get there and (2) and what I would find if, and when, I got there, always focused on immediate tasks at hand (namely, data collection and ways of making it more reliable and more efficient).

In the late 1990s, I saw some first, tentative results from the *Il Lavoro* database. The technology was simply too crude and too cumbersome for a smooth transition from words to numbers. Ten more years passed. I created another database from *Avanti!* and then from *Il Popolo d'Italia*. Even after the completion of data collection from *Avanti!* and *Il Popolo d'Italia*, I had to develop more tools to query the information in easy and quick ways for data analysis. In the spring of 2008, the *Avanti!* results started pouring in quickly. And they were amazing (although, for sure, no "giant step for mankind"). If someone had asked me, in 1982, "What would you ideally like to see at the end of this journey 'from words to numbers'?" I could not have wished for more. In January 2008, I saw the results of network analyses. On March 15, I saw the first set of GIS maps. The beauty of those maps, on top of the previous network graphs, made it for me a very emotional day (a day that ended even more dramatically, caught on the road in the tornado that hit Atlanta that night, with trees and rooftops, windows, and garbage cans flying in the air and hitting the car, and all seemed lost). Jesse Hamner, who witnessed the outpouring of those emotions, put it to me cogently: "It is nice to see technology catch up to one's dream."

Acknowledgments

The writing of this book benefited from help from several individuals and institutions. Tim Liao, the Series Editor, supported the project and patiently waited for its delivery. The data analyzed in this book were collected with grants from the University of Reading, University of Trento (where Gianfranco Poggi made available his unspent personal research funds; *grazie!*), Emory University, and Provincia Autonoma di Trento. Many students worked for several years as coders, in particular Elisa Forestan, Gloria Albertini, Liana Carpenè, Elisa Fracalossi, Giorgia Giardino, Silvia Girardi, Alessandra Onofrio, and Manuel Rauzi. Data collection was carried out at the Faculty of Sociology of the University of Trento. Antonio Chiesi, Mario Diani, Gustavo Corni, and Renato Mazzolini made this possible. Luigi Lissandrini and Alberto Sanna from IT Services at Trento provided invaluable support. Trento gave warm hospitality not just to my project but to me personally. I have left behind many good friends. The Windows version of PC-ACE was implemented by Benedict Elliott-Smith and extended by Fabio Cunial (with a great deal of programming on my part). PC-ACE development was supported by the Nuffield Foundation, University of Reading, University of Trento, Emory University, and Provincia Autonoma di Trento. My research assistant, Gianluca De Fazio, helped with data aggregation and data extraction for various types of statistical analysis. Michael Page (IT Services at Emory) prepared the GIS maps (with the help of Rob O'Reilly and Jesse Hamner, also from Emory IT Services). Claude Rubinson ran the QCA analyses, and Ivano Bison performed the sequence and event history analyses. Sophie Doyle and Stefania Vicari made available some of the findings from their dissertation work. Jana Diesner (from AutoMap), Sophie Doyle, Susanne Friese (from ATLAS.ti), and Stefania Vicari provided software help. The writing of the book benefited from teaching quantitative narrative analysis at the ECPR Summer School in Ljubljana in 2006 and 2007 and at the Oslo Summer School in Comparative Social Science Studies in 2008, where Bernhard Kittel and Benoît Rihoux (ECPR Summer School), and Lars Mjøset (Oslo Summer School) invited me. Participants in these courses contributed to the book with questions and ideas. Robert Biggert, Morten Baender, Selina Cruz-Charrez, Gianluca De Fazio, Simone Ledermann, John Markoff, Orlando Martinez-Garcia, Mila Mikalayeva, and Stefania

Vicari provided helpful comments on different drafts of the book. In the end, just when I thought I was done and could do no better with the manuscript, Rüya Gökhan Koçer (University of Amsterdam) and Tammy Smith (SUNY Stony Brook), the two SAGE reviewers, Pierpaolo Mudu, and Tim Liao, the Series Editor, provided further comments that were invaluable. At different times of this journey, deans Dianne Berry at the University of Reading and Robert Paul at Emory generously contributed research funds and leave time for the project and for the book.

Last but not least, without Charles Tilly and Aaron Cicourel this journey of going from words to numbers or of quantifying narrative would not have been possible. From Charles Tilly, I learned to take the first steps—and much more. This book is gratefully dedicated to his memory. Aaron Cicourel was the anonymous reviewer of my first paper on the technique eventually published in 1989 in *Sociological Methodology* whom I acknowledged with the following words in my other book *From Words to Numbers*: "Perhaps, s/he may never know how deeply her/his review changed the course of my intellectual and professional trajectory." He now knows.

To all these people and institutions goes my gratitude for making this book and my entire journey from words to numbers possible.

List of Figures

List of Tables

List of Equations

To Chuck Tilly, mentor and friend

Semper dum vivam, tui meminero.

Of journeys: Don't travel too close to home. You are unlikely to find much that is novel and different from what you know, however solitary and risky new paths may be. Yet all travel starts from where you are. And starting from home, you can get very far, there where home is no longer a place you can see. In the end, your entire route will have been marked by your starting point, even when you may have encountered many crisscrossing roads along the way.

CHAPTER 1. ORIENTATION

Abstract

Words *or* numbers. Quality *or* quantity. Better, words *against* numbers. Quality *against* quantity. The debate (a war of words) has long raged in the social sciences, leaving scholars divided into fiercely opposing camps. Yet qualitative scholars often use quantitative expressions (imprecisely and without much rigor via qualitative quantifiers), and quantitative scholars conveniently forget that often the words are right below the surface of their numbers (if they care to scratch). Indeed, some of the measures quantitative social scientists use are born as numbers (e.g., tonnage of ships, miles of railroad built, industrial production), but others become numbers as counts of what are essentially words. Standard quantitative measures such as crime statistics, labor statistics, or strike data are nothing but counts of specific types of events originally expressed in words in police or newspaper reports or in survey questions.[1] Survey research, a quintessential quantitative social science technique, constructs its numbers by counting prepackaged answers to prepackaged questions (and then forgets the words on which these counts are based).

This book takes a different approach to the problem of measurement and social scientific explanation. It proposes a method of investigation that turns words into numbers but does so without reneging on its origins, without turning its back on the words—whatever the source of these words: newspaper accounts of events, field notes, or transcripts of in-depth interviews. It exploits some fundamental linguistic properties of a specific type of text (narrative) to build a method that ultimately allows one to go "from words to numbers," to extract numbers out of words. And those numbers, being based on linguistic properties of narrative rather than on the investigator's theoretical interests, are as hypothesis free as the current state of the art of measurement can deliver. In keeping with the roots of the technique in linguistics and literary theory, it does not turn *against* the words once the words have yielded the numbers. Rather, it tries to take advantage of the best properties of both words and numbers.

2

Question and Answer (How Can You Study Stories?)

Consider this newspaper article. It appeared in the Italian socialist paper *Avanti!* on April 1, 1921:

> Lucca's Labor Chamber Destroyed. Last night, around 10 pm, a group of fascists, crossing the city walls that lead from the fortress of San Martino to that of San Paolino, where the Labor Chamber is located, knocked down the entrance door and the internal side ones, breaking all the furniture and removing documents and red flags, and a poster with "Labor Chamber" written on it. Then, the fascists went to the headquarters of the Socialist Youth Club, located in via Boccherini. Unable to get in through the main door, they tore down a wall and once inside they destroyed all the furniture and various portraits, and removed all the documents. Some gunshots were fired in the air. Heading for the Railway Workers' Union, the fascists found it guarded by police, and unable to get in, they went to the custodian's home (who didn't answer). Police, continuing in their zealous and precious job of defending the law equally for everyone, except for the socialists, arrested some fifteen socialists belonging to the Workers' Leagues and unsympathetic to Fascism. Talking about justice! (p. 1, column 4).

The article is one of several thousand published by *Avanti!* between 1919 and 1922 on the violent events that led to Mussolini's seizure of power in October 1922 and to 20 years of fascist dictatorship in Italy. It tells us of social actors, of their behavior, of the targets of their actions, of time and place. It tells us a story.

Question
Confronted with thousands of articles, with thousands of stories, is there a way of using, as data, *all* the information they provide other than simply counting events? Are there characteristics of stories that are invariant across different stories and that can be used in systematic ways to study the sociohistorical events described in the stories?

Answer
Yes, there are invariant characteristics of narrative. A handful of linguists and literary critics chipped away at stories in search of these invariant characteristics. And their findings happened very quickly. The English translation of Vladimir Propp's *Morphology of the Folktale,* first published in Russian in 1928, appeared in the United States in 1958. A few years later, in 1966, both Greimas's *Semantique Structurale* and a special issue of the journal *Communications* entirely dedicated to narrative under the title "Recherches sémiologiques. L'Analyse structurale du récit" appeared in France. The issue of *Communications* that contained this article also contained some of the seminal contributions to the structural analysis of narrative by Bremond, Todorov, and

others, especially, Barthes's introductory essay, "Introduction à l'analyse structurale des récits." By the early 1970s, all major works on narrative had appeared in print on both sides of the Atlantic, including Labov's work, with its classification of the functional parts of narrative as orientation, complication, evaluation, resolution, and coda (Labov, 1972; Labov & Waletzky, 1967). Under the influence of structuralism, all these works sought to identify the invariant, structural properties of narrative. "A narrative," Barthes (1966/1977, p. 80) wrote, "shares with other narratives a common structure which is open to analysis, no matter how much patience its formulation requires." There has been a steady stream of work in search of that common structure, of "the invariant structural units which are represented by a variety of superficial forms," of the recurrent characteristics and the "distinguishable *regularities*" behind narrative, behind the "millions of narratives," namely, the sequential ordering of narrative clauses, the story-versus-plot distinction of this sequential ordering, and the basic structure of narrative clauses as actors and their actions in time and space.[2]

This book exploits the findings of that tradition. And, no doubt unforeseen by the early contributors, mostly located in the fields of linguistics and literary criticism, it takes their insights one step further, to turn words into numbers. It starts from the structural, invariant categories of narrative in terms of sequences of actors and their actions in time and space; then, it places these relational categories in a computer environment—more specifically, in a relational database management system (RDBMS); it fills these empty categories with the appropriate words taken from thousands of "real" narratives of sociohistorical events; through counting, it turns all these words into numbers; and, finally, it analyzes these numbers with the help of a variety of both traditional and novel statistical techniques.

The tradition this book draws on is very different from the quantitative approach to texts that has been dominant in the social sciences: content analysis (Franzosi, 2004a, 2008; Krippendorf, 1980; Weber, 1990). The fundamental difference between quantitative narrative analysis (QNA) and content analysis, in its multiple variants, is that the categories of QNA are based on linguistic properties of texts—narrative texts in particular—as drawn from a literary and linguistic tradition that has worked long and hard at teasing out those properties. Content analysis, on the other hand, bases its categories on the investigator's theoretical and/or substantive interests. In content analysis, categories vary from investigator to investigator, from subfield to subfield, although some sedimentation of categories is inevitable *within* subfields as new investigators address previous scholarly work. QNA is different from content analysis even when, by sheer chance, content analysis ends up adopting the same categories of quantitative narrative analysis, simply because the type of text used as source of data to be coded is fundamentally a narrative (that is the case, for instance, with Protest Event Analysis; see Koopmans & Rucht, 2002).

What content analysis and quantitative narrative analysis have in common, however, is the drive to quantify, to use words for the purpose of extracting numbers out of them, something foreign to the linguistic tradition of narrative analysis. The invariant linguistic properties of narrative on which QNA is based, however, help deliver more hypothesis-free data than content analysis, with its coding schemes based on investigators' theoretical interests. Grounding my work in the tradition of linguistic and literary criticism helps spell out both advantages and disadvantages of the approach illustrated in this book (e.g., it works well only with narrative-type texts). It also helps make clear the connection between words and numbers and between specific properties of narrative and specific types of statistical analyses.

In a nutshell, these are the things we learn in this book: What narrative is and how to use its categories for the purpose of quantifying narrative information. To put it differently, we will learn how to go from words to numbers, in a journey that will take us across different disciplines, from linguistics and literary criticism to computer science and statistics.

"Words Are Beautiful: Why Turn Them Into Numbers?"

Question
Words are beautiful: Why do you want to turn them into numbers?

Answer
This question has been put to me, after public presentations, in exactly those words. Why, indeed, should we turn words into numbers? There are many learned answers to this question, across a number of disciplines, from sociology to political science and history (on the drive toward quantification, see Franzosi, 2004b, pp. 279–285, 301–307). Lasswell (1949, p. 52) himself raised the question "why be quantitative?" with specific reference to content analysis. His answer was, "Because of the scientific and policy gains that can come of it". No doubt the patterns revealed by the statistical analyses of the chapter "Things to Do with Words" would be unthinkable in the realm of words. Based on some 18,000 documents and 140,000 semantic triplets (or skeleton narrative sentences), there would simply be too many words for any of us to be able to juggle them meaningfully in our heads. So the answer to the question "why turn words into numbers?" depends on the number of words. Indeed, words are beautiful . . . in small doses. The manipulation of numbers is far easier since it can be

done via specialized statistical software (although . . . it wasn't long ago that computers were human and the handling of numbers was just as difficult as that of words; see Grier, 2005).

Indeed, quantification partly results from the amount of material available. Historian Arnold Toynbee (1946) provides the following explanation for the old Aristotelian distinction in the techniques of history, science, and fiction:

> [T]he techniques of history, science and fiction . . . differ from each other in their suitability for dealing with "data" of different quantities. The ascertainment and record of particular facts is all that is possible in a field of study where the data happen to be few. The elucidation and formulation of laws is both possible and necessary where the data are too numerous to tabulate but not too numerous to survey. . . . [F]iction is the only technique that can be employed or is worth employing where the data are innumerable. . . . The techniques differ in their utility for handling different quantities of data. (pp. 45–46)

In line with this Aristotelian distinction, I make no presumption on the superiority of a quantitative approach to narrative texts. I quantify simply because I have far too much information to deal with qualitatively.

The Fundamental Dilemma

And yet can I get away that easily from making a choice between quality and quantity, with "no presumption on the superiority of a quantitative approach to narrative texts"? In the early 1600s, the members of one the first European academies of science—the Italian Academy of the Lynx (of which Galileo was a proud member)—best expressed that dilemma and tension. As David Freedberg (2002) put it, in a magisterial reconstruction of the Academy's work in botany and zoology based on the pictorial representation of species and their classification:

> On the one hand: pictures, with all their potential for descriptive density, and their capacity to record every detail and all creatures in their full anomalousness. On the other hand: diagrams, with their capacity to abstract, to reduce things to their essentials, to show basic relationships between things and within the things themselves. What is at stake is more than a simple polarity. It is a drama that plays itself out over and over again in the history of the reproduction and dissemination of scientific knowledge. (p. 397)

Substitute for the word *picture* in this passage the word *event* or *narrative event* and you relive that drama as portrayed in the pages of this book: Greater and greater in-depth narrative detail and richness on an event may not get us an inch closer to the fundamental problem of finding out what different narrative events have in common.[3]

6

Road Map

This book is divided into five chapters. The first chapter, a brief "Orientation" (you are already halfway through it), sets the terrain that we need to cover in this journey. In the next chapter, "Text Genres, Narrative, and Story Grammar," I show that narrative is a distinctive text genre, that is, a type of text with distinctive properties different from those of other texts.[4] In particular, narrative is characterized by a sequence of events, where these events are centered on (mostly) human actors performing some actions in relation to other actors. The sequence of the actor-action-actor structures is invariant in narrative. Furthermore, these sequences must be coherent and must have a point, the point often providing a justification. With the use of linguistic rules, I show how to map formally narrative into this invariant structure with actors and their characteristics (as syntactic subjects), actions and their characteristics (in particular, time and space, but also reason, outcome, instrument), pro or against other actors with their characteristics (as syntactic complements or objects). This Subject-Action-Object (SAO) structure provides a sort of "story grammar." In its most essential elements, it is equivalent to the 5-W structure of journalism: who, what, when, where, why, and how. I argue that quantitative narrative analysis provides a far more rigorous research tool than content analysis, the traditional social science quantitative approach to texts.

In the next chapter, "Computer Storage and Retrieval of Narrative Information," I show how to implement a story grammar in a computer environment. Story grammars are simply too complex for paper and pencil. Without software, the use of story grammars would be relegated to trivial and exemplary applications. I review various software options, from automatic approaches (e.g., KEDS, IDEA) to software based on the SAO structure (e.g., ETHNO, AutoMap). I explore ways of doing quantitative narrative analysis in commercially available computer-assisted qualitative data analysis software (CAQDAS, e.g., ATLAS.ti, N6, NVivo, MAXQDA, WinMax). Although CAQDAS programs are better suited for thematic content analysis, I show ways of implementing a simple story grammar in ATLAS.ti (these software packages all work in very similar ways; for a hands-on, step-by-step comparison of this type of software, see Lewins & Silver, 2007; for an in-depth comparison in relation to QNA, see Franzosi, Doyle, McClelland, Rankin, & Vicari, 2009). Given the limited applicability of available software for quantitative narrative analysis, I show how to implement a story grammar within relational database management systems (RDBMS). These systems are ideally suited to implementing a story grammar, given the relational properties of story grammars. I highlight the features of RDBMS database design for a quantitative approach to narrative based on story grammars and illustrate an RDBMS software package that I specifically developed to carry out QNA (PC-ACE, Program for Computer-Assisted Coding of Events, available for free download at www.pc-ace.com). I use data that I collected from newspapers via PC-ACE on the rise of Italian fascism (1919–1922) (but I also illustrate different substantive applications).

In the chapter "Things to Do With Words," you learn how to analyze statistically the thousands of words you have stored in a computer. After all, words can be counted and, through counting, turned into numbers, and numbers can be analyzed statistically. Although traditional statistical techniques can be used with QNA data (e.g., factor analysis and regression analysis), the emphasis is on techniques that have a clear correspondence with fundamental properties of narrative, in particular network analysis, event history analysis, geographic information system (GIS) tools, and sequence analysis. Indeed, if narrative, at the linguistic level, is about actors doing certain actions (including "speech acts," in actions of saying), perhaps in favor or against other actors, then network analysis is an ideal tool of statistical analysis, focused as it is on bringing out networks of social interaction. If time and space are the fundamental categories of narrative (as underscored by the way stories start in many languages, "Once upon a time" or "Once upon a time, in a kingdom at the far end of the earth"), then we need to look for statistical analyses centered on time and/or space. Several types of statistical models deal with time as the main indexing mechanism for their variables (from spectral analysis to econometric models). But event history analysis bases its analyses on the time of events and their duration—properties of narrative. Similarly, if sequences of narrative clauses provide the running cloth of narrative, then sequence analysis could help tease out that fabric. Finally, GIS tools (still little used in the social sciences) are fundamentally based on the knowledge of location (along with time, actors, and their actions). GIS can be used to map in space and time the distribution/diffusion of actions (the A part of the SAO structure, with the time and space attributes).

In "Coda," the final chapter, we learn some of the tricks of the trade, to borrow Becker's (1998) expression. As in all trades, there are many little tricks in QNA you'd better know beforehand to make your life easier and avoid costly surprises. We go over the limits of the approach, one more time. QNA will serve you well if you know its limitations and not just its power.

You and I: The Book and Its Audience

Going "from words to numbers" via QNA requires some familiarity with a combination of disciplines not usually found together in the social scientist's tool kit: linguistics, computer science, and statistics. For an introductory text such as this one, the danger is of losing some readers and boring the others. Readers with a linguistics background may find it hard to negotiate their way through network models and Markov chains (and, vice versa, readers with statistical training may not easily digest the linguists' and literary critics' jargon on narrative). Building a database relying on the handful of pages on database design provided in the book is probably out of the question for the novice. I make no attempt to explain the mathematical foundations of network, GIS, or sequence models. I simply show why (and how) some tools are ideally suited to analyzing narrative data, the kind of patterns they can reveal. All this, within the page limits of the "Quantitative Applications in the Social Sciences" series.

Of necessity, I flee hurriedly from one topic to the next, providing just enough information to show how QNA works, what questions it allows one to answer. Thus, the sections on narrative may give an intelligent reader the basis for understanding differences between different types of texts, what narrative is, and how its invariant characteristics can be used for a systematic approach to narrative texts. The scanty pages on database design—certainly not sufficient for anyone to build a database—may provide enough of a basis for understanding SQL (Structured Query Language) and how to extract the complex information stored in a database in easy and flexible ways.

To complicate matters further, none of the popular, commercially available CAQDAS (e.g., ATLAS.ti, NVivo, MAXQDA, WinMax) allows a full implementation of QNA. Thus, I rely on PC-ACE, a program that I specifically developed to carry out QNA, to illustrate the use of QNA (after all, no software, no QNA). Yet this book is not intended as a primer for PC-ACE (PC-ACE comes with a sample database and an extensive user manual that, step-by-step, leads users through the various options available). For this reason, I do engage other software. Given the popularity of some of these software options, they would probably be the first port of call of anyone interested in computer-assisted analysis of narrative. These computer programs do offer ways of carrying out QNA, unfortunately limited.

No doubt I only whet the reader's appetite. I hope that the book provides enough information for a reader to get the gist of the approach and enough introductory and intermediate-level references to allow curious readers to pursue topics of interest.

The target reader of the book is thus a social scientist or a historian (rather than a linguist or computer scientist). More specifically, he or she is a social scientist with a quantitative bent in social explanation and the curiosity (or need) of finding out what to do with large volumes of textual data, narrative data in particular. A qualitative social scientist may have a harder time with the chapters on computer science and statistics (perhaps, with the very raison d'être of the book—turning words into numbers— why?). Yet even this reader may find of interest what words, in particular large volumes of words, can reveal about sociohistorical reality when dealt with in specific, systematic ways (ways different from the just as systematic ones with which qualitative narrative analysis or discourse analysis approach texts). After all, many of the texts qualitative researchers deal with—field notes, transcripts of in-depth interviews and focus groups, and, especially, oral and life histories—contain narratives of people's lives. Regardless of specific research needs, the book may be an ideal assignment in a course on methods of social research, given QNA's commitment to straddle quality and quantity, to combine quality *with* quantity, rather than pitch quality *against* quantity.

A Word on Style

Several sections and subsections of the book are very short. I have used this typographic approach intentionally to draw attention to issues and topics. There are many lessons strewn throughout the book, all at a quick pace. I want to make sure they don't get lost, the very table of contents serving as a reminder. Some section titles echo the work of others (e.g., Orientation, Coda, Things to Do With Words). Other titles ask rhetorical questions (you have already seen one in this introduction). Again, this is not accidental. I use this approach throughout the book. There is a long tradition in rhetoric of the use of "rhetorical questions" (generally known under the technical name of *erotema*) and with different technical names depending on the goal of the question and answer, from *anthypophora* to *anacoenosis, dianoea, aporia,* and more. Although no longer a popular form of writing, I deemed it appropriate for an introductory text, as an old-fashioned approach to its modern counterpart, the FAQ (Frequently Asked Questions). Indeed, the questions asked (and the answers given) are not just rhetorical, hypothetical questions but "real" questions frequently asked by first-time users of either PC-ACE or QNA. The rhetorical reliance on erotema brings with it a more direct relationship between reader and author, between you and me. Authors and readers are *never* directly acknowledged in modern scientific writing (as underscored by the use of passive forms; on these issues, see Franzosi, 2004b, pp. 194–214).

Enough! Let's hurry along, our road map at hand.

Notes

1. From these counts, ratios are often constructed, such as the unemployment or crime rate, constructed, respectively, as the ratio between the count of people unemployed divided by the count of people in the labor force or the count of people who have suffered a crime over the total population in a city, state, or country.

2. Respectively, Labov and Waletzky (1967, p. 12), Greimas (1971, p. 794), and Barthes (1966/1977, p. 81).

3. Although it may well help suggest more and more relationships (see Freedberg's repeated references to the Linceans's dilemma, 2002, pp. 5, 48, 179–183, 284–286, 291–292, 300, 304, 349–356, 366, 384–393, 397, 399, 410, 412).

4. Definitions and taxonomies of genre are contested terrain in genre theory (genres, indeed, vary from comedy vs. tragedy, depending on the ultimate ending of a sequence of events, to narrative vs. procedural, expository, hortatory, and descriptive, depending on the speaker's/writer's intent). I have adopted a loose approach to simply denote a class of texts with distinctive and invariant characteristics.

CHAPTER 2. TEXT GENRES, NARRATIVE, AND STORY GRAMMARS

Story and Narrative (What the Linguists Say)

In one of American sociology's classics, Thomas and Znaniecki's (1918) *The Polish Peasant in Europe and America*, we read this letter sent by Konstancya Walerych, a young Polish immigrant to America, to her parents.

> Dearest parents, I inform you that I received the letter sent by you from which I got information about your health and success also. As to myself, thanks to God the Highest, I am in good health, which I wish also to you from all my heart. As to my success, it is not very good because I have done housework, and have been paid $10 for this month, but I had too heavy work; I was obliged to work too long. Now, dearest parents, I inform you that I have at present no work and I don't know what will be further. Dearest parents, you ask to be informed where I have been boarding after coming to America. I was with my sister and now I am with my sister. Dearest parents, don't be angry with me for not sending you anything up to the present, but I inform you that I could not, because when I traveled to America I remained for a week in Antwerp, and when I came to America I had no work for three weeks, and you know well, dearest parents, that I did not come to parents here; in America nothing is to be had without paying.[1] (p. 474; letter dated December 8, 1913, Greenburg, PA)

In her letter, Konstancya briefly tells her parents back home the story of her life after leaving Poland for America, with deep insights on American society: stopping in Antwerp for a week, arriving in America, boarding with her sister, being unemployed, then working long hours doing housework, and being unemployed again.

But what is a story? A story, according to the *Oxford English Dictionary* (OED, 1989) is

> A narrative, true or presumed to be true, relating to important events and celebrated persons of a more or less remote past; a historical relation or anecdote.

> A recital of events that have or are alleged to have happened; a series of events that are or might be narrated.

A narrative of real or, more usually, fictitious events, designed for the entertainment of the hearer or reader; a series of traditional or imaginary incidents forming the matter of such a narrative; a tale.

Story and narrative thus seem to go hand in hand. Indeed, the same *OED* defines *narrative* as "An account or narration; a history, tale, story, recital (of facts, etc.)." Poem, letter, children's book, or newspaper article, for as long as they tell a story, they constitute narrative, regardless of text genre. As Barthes (1966/1977) put it,

> Narrative is present in myth, legend, fable, tale, novella, epic, history, tragedy, drama, comedy, mime, painting (think of Carpaccio's *Saint Ursula*), stained glass windows, cinema, comics, news item, conversation. Moreover, under this almost infinite diversity of forms, narrative is present in every age, in every place, in every society; it begins with the very history of mankind and there nowhere is nor has been a people without narrative. All classes, all human groups, have their narratives . . . narrative is international, transhistorical, transcultural: it is simply there, like life itself. (p. 79)

Beyond the *OED* definitions, the key ingredients of story, narrative, and series of events are all found among linguists and literary critics as well. For Labov (1972), "narrative . . . [is] one method of recapitulating past experience by matching a verbal sequence of clauses to the sequence of events which [it is inferred] actually occurred." "A *minimal narrative*," Labov continues, "[is] a sequence of two clauses which are *temporally ordered* . . . The skeleton of a narrative . . . consists of a series of temporally ordered clauses" (pp. 359–361). Rimmon-Kenan (1983) defines "narrative . . . [as] a *succession of events*" (pp. 2–3). "The distinguishing feature of narrative," Cohan and Shires write (1988), "is its linear organization of events" (pp. 52–53). For Toolan (1988), "A minimalist definition of narrative might be: a perceived sequence of non-randomly connected events" (p. 7).[2] For Gérard Genette (1972/1980), "narrative refer(s) to the succession of events, real or fictitious" (p. 26).

All these definitions of narrative stress the idea of sequence or succession of events. Tomashevski, Labov, Prince, Bal, Todorov, Rimmon-Kenan, Cohan, and Shires all drum that same point away.[3] And that point goes back to the Russian formalists of the beginning of the 20th century, Propp and Tomashevski in particular, if not to Aristotle, for whom plot-structure (*mythos*) meant "the organisation of the events" (Halliwell, 1987, p. 37). It is the Russian formalists who, in the 1920s, introduced the distinction between story and plot in narrative (*fabula* vs. *sjužet*). For Tomashevski (1925/1965, p. 67), "plot [*sjužet*] is distinct from story [*fabula*]. Both include the same events, but in the plot the events *are arranged* and connected according to the orderly sequence in which they were presented in the work." The plot, in other words, refers to the way events are presented by the author to the reader.[4] The *story* refers to a skeleton description of the fundamental events in their chronological order (perhaps with an equally skeleton listing of the roles of the characters in the story) (Bal, 1977, p. 4; Toolan, 1988, p. 9).

The French structuralists preserved that distinction between story and plot, *fabula* and *sjužet,* gave it the labels *histoire* and *discours,*[5] story versus discourse, and further divided the plot/discourse level into *text* (or, more generally, discourse) and narrating or *narration* (Genette, 1972/1980, p. 27; Toolan, 1988, pp. 10–11). It is the story—the chronological succession of events—that provides the essential building blocks of narrative. Without story, there is no narrative (Rimmon-Kenan, 1983, p. 15). A story implies a change in situations as expressed by the unfolding of a specific sequence of events (Tomashevski, 1965, p. 70). The events in the story must disrupt an initial state of equilibrium setting in motion an inversion of situation, a change of fortunes: from good to bad, from bad to good.[6] In classical Aristotelian poetics, the turn of fortunes—a *reversal*—is the key characteristic of comedy and tragedy (Halliwell, 1987, p. 42).[7] Whereas comedy marks an improvement of a situation, tragedy marks its worsening. Reversals can occur repeatedly in a story along the sequence: initial state → disruption → new state → disruption → new state → . . . → final state (equilibrium). Each new state is both a point of arrival and a point of departure, a sort of temporary equilibrium between the before and after, the past and the future (Todorov, 1978/1990, p. 30).

"The inversion of an event is one of the essential features of a story," sums up Prince (1973, p. 28). Another essential feature is the temporal ordering of events in a story, the chronological sequence of actions/events. In a sequence, not all events are as equally consequential for a change of situation. Aristotle said as much in his *Poetics:* "it makes a great difference whether things happen because of one another, or only *after* one another" (Halliwell, trans., 1987, p. 42). This distinction between those actions and events that fundamentally alter a narrative situation and the ones that don't, between sequential and consequential actions, is still recurrent in the field.[8] Consequential actions have been variously called *dynamic motifs* (Tomashevski, 1925/1965, p. 70), *cardinal functions* (or *nuclei*; Barthes, 1977, pp. 93–94), and *kernels* (Chatman, 1978, pp. 32, 53–56; Rimmon-Kenan, 1983, p. 16), whereas sequential actions are *static motifs, catalyzers,* and *satellites.* Deletion of consequential actions would fundamentally destroy the narrative logic (Chatman, 1978, p. 53). These actions open up narrative choices. This way, narrative sequences imply causal sequences; narration implies causation.[9]

Narrative Functions, Sequences, and Invariant Structures of Narrative

For Propp, the core actions of a story (more specifically, of Russian folktales, the stories he studied) and their sequence form an invariant structure. Regardless of the particular content of a folktale, regardless of how the story is told, all Russian folktales, according to Propp, exhibit (at least some of) 31 basic "functions," where functions are actions of a tale, "an act of a character" (Propp, 1928/1968, p. 21; e.g., the appearance of a villain through the functions of "violation" and "villainy," the "counteraction" of the hero and his "departure," the hero's "struggle" with the villain and his "victory" over the villain, the hero's "return" and his "wedding"). As Propp (1928/1968) put it, "The number of functions is extremely small, whereas the number of personages is extremely large. This explains the twofold quality of a tale: its amazing multiformity, picturesqueness, and color, and on the other hand, its no less striking uniformity, its repetition" (pp. 20–21).

Greimas (1966, 1971) further aggregated Propp's 31 functions into a set of five functions: (1) disruption of a state of equilibrium; (2) arrival and mission of the hero; (3) trial of the hero; (4) task accomplished by the hero; and (5) return to the original state of equilibrium.[10] Colby, in his study of Eskimo folktales, focuses on three main classes of narrative actions, "motivation," "engagement," and "resolution," each, in its turn, consisting of several lower-level elements (that he calls *eidons*), which are similar to Propp's functions.[11]

Labov (1972, pp. 362–370; see also Labov & Waletzky, 1967) found a six-part macrostructure in vernacular narratives of New York Harlem African Americans: abstract, orientation, complicating action, evaluation, result or resolution, and coda.[12] Of these six functional parts, the complicating action, usually made up of a series of events, is both necessary and sufficient to constitute a narrative (Labov, 1972, p. 370; Labov & Waletzky, 1967, p. 32).[13]

Coherence and Story Point: "There Is No Free Lunch in America"

Actions and their sequence thus seem to be defining characteristics of narrative. Yet not every sequence of any two temporally ordered actions/events constitutes a narrative, gives you a story (Rimmon-Kenan, 1983,

p. 19). Take these two "narrative sentences" (Danto, 1985, p. 143): "Paul got up at 7 a.m. His son Mike got up half an hour later." Although temporally sequenced, the two sentences do not, by themselves, constitute a story. "So what?" the reader would probably ask if confronted with the text. And if nothing else followed, that same reader would most likely try to fill the missing gaps, making up the rest of the story: "After getting dressed and having breakfast, they walked to school together (or they went to the park, or they drove to the stadium)." The temporal ordering of actions/events in a story is a necessary but not sufficient condition for the emergence of a story. The events in the sequence must also be meaningful overall (coherence). There must also be a point to the story.[14]

Let us go back to the letter that Konstancya Walerych, the Polish immigrant to America we met earlier, wrote to her parents. It is not hard to recognize this text as narrative. After all, the text deals with "the temporal character of human experience," as Ricoeur (1984, p. 52) would require of narrative or, to state the same idea through Labov (1972, p. 359), the text deals with the "recapitulation of past experience." It involves a change in situation (from living at home with her parents in Poland to being on her own in America). It contains both narrative and nonnarrative (mostly evaluative) clauses arranged in chronological order (see Table 2.1).

Table 2.1 Chronological Sequence of Narrative Sentences in Konstancya Walerych's Letter

t_1	Konstancya Walerych leaves Poland to emigrate to America
t_2	Konstancya does not send any money (and continues not to do so to the present) to her parents
t_3	Konstancya has a 1-week stopover in Antwerp on the way to America
t_4	Konstancya arrives in America
t_5	Konstancya lives (and continues to do so at the time of writing) with her sister on arrival in America
t_6	Konstancya cannot find work for 3 weeks after arriving
t_7	Konstancya works as a household cleaner
t_8	Konstancya receives a letter from her parents in Poland
t_9	Konstancya loses her job and has no job at present
t_{10}	Konstancya writes to her parents in Poland

The entries in Table 2.1 give us the story—the ingredients (events in chronological order, t_1 through t_{10}) out of which Konstancya Walerych fashions her plot. And that plot, notwithstanding the simplicity of language and sentence construction (a marker of an uneducated narrator), is very effective. She starts her letter with the event of t_8 and follows with several descriptive clauses about the parents' health and success, her own health and success (or lack of success), her hard work at low pay. Most narrative sentences contained in the text (t_2, t_{10}) come in rapid succession at the very end of the letter, building a dramatic finale about her inability to send money home, not because she has forgotten them—the term *dearest parents* appears five times in a short text, her wishes of good health come "from all my heart," "don't be angry with me"—but because life for her has been marred by simply too many difficulties. The whole letter is a justification for not helping her parents back home, the personal story point. But the letter also contains an important "sociological" story point, the result of an amazing cultural observation of a new immigrant: "in America nothing is to be had without paying." Even family relations change in America; Konstancya "did not come to parents" (but to a sister; the implication is that she has had to pay for her hospitality). There is, after all, no free lunch in America!

Justification

The evaluation contained in Konstancya's letter is altogether typical of narrative. According to Labov, the sequential organization of events provides the most important aspect of narrative—the referential function of narrative—but narratives are also characterized by a second function—the evaluative function (Labov, 1972; Labov & Waletzky, 1967). Basically, the first function addresses the question "What is the story?" (sequence of events). The second function deals with the question "Why is the story told?" (story point; e.g., see Toolan, 1988, p. 147). The more complex the story, the more likely that it will explicitly satisfy the evaluative function with one or multiple story points. Evaluation goes hand in hand with justification. By telling her parents that "in America nothing is to be had without paying," including hospitality by her own sister, even when she had no job, Konstancya is justifying the fact that she hasn't sent any money home (as expected by Old World family relations).

But fashioning a coherent story, with a point to the story, ultimately involves a careful selection of facts. Any fact that does not fit the particular story and its point will have to be dropped. Our academic CVs—or, more generally, biographies—are good examples (and ones that will strike familiar chords; what goes in and what's left out). Even the simplest of narratives, such as Konstancya Walerych's letter, display skillful backgrounding and foregrounding of information that, implicitly or explicitly, ideologically color a text. As Skinner has argued, the process of production of text is always inextricably linked to the production of ideology.[15] Even the referential function of narrative—the chronological sequence of narrative clauses—is not devoid of evaluation. Purely narrative sequences are never innocent. Konstancya's story (as opposed to plot) ends at times t_9 and t_{10}, when she writes to her parents after losing her job. It leaves the reader with a final moral justification for not sending money home.

Events

By now, it should be clear. A narrative subsumes a story (and a plot); and this is based on a sequential organization of events, where each individual element of the sequence can be simply sequential or consequential and the sequence as a whole has a teleological end in the story point.

But what is an event? Despite the central role of this concept in any definition of narrative, story, and plot, you will be hard-pressed to find a rigorous definition of *event* in the vast body of literature on narrative. The event almost seems to be taken as a given, as a commonsensical element of the language that does not need to be defined. After all, would you think of defining *a* or *the* or even *sequence*? Rimmon-Kenan (1983) relies "without great rigour" on the *OED* definition of *event* as a "thing that happens" (p. 2) and since "when something happens, the situation usually changes. An event, then, may be said to be a change from one state of affairs to another" (p. 15). Toolan (1988), whose *Narrative: A Critical Linguistic Introduction* is full of useful definitions, is rather vague about the key term *event*, a term he puts in bold to mark its significance but then simply states, "[The] **event** itself is a complex term, presupposing that there is some recognized state or set of conditions, and that *something happens,* causing a change of that state" (p. 7).

What is this "thing," this "something" that happens? For Rimmon-Kenan (1983), the "something that happens, [is] something that can be summed up by a verb or a *name of action* [italics added]" (p. 2). Bremond (1966) talks of story as "a succession of events of *human interest* subsumed under the same *action* [italics added]" (p. 102). For Todorov (1971/1977), a story "evokes a certain reality, events that one presumes took place, characters that, from that point of view, are confused with those of real life" (p. 231). And let's not forget the definition of Labov, for whom "narrative . . . [is] one method of recapitulating past experience" (1972, p. 359) (one's experience, human experience).

18

Implicitly, then, what narrative theorists have in mind when they talk about events is *human action*. Other types of events (and characters) can be part of narrative but only in a subordinate position (e.g., a heat wave and the effect that global warming may have on the probability of this type of event). They don't play a leading role but only a supportive one (e.g., in a story of older people having to be hospitalized during the heat wave). Similarly, description and evaluation do not constitute an integral part of narrative. "In general, narrative theorists rather tend to analyse the course of action to which they limit their *story*" (Bal, 1977, p. 89). As Toolan (1988) writes, "What is said . . . will not be the core of a story; that, rather, what is done . . . will be. The 'what is done' then becomes (or may become) the core narrative text of clauses—actions—while the 'what is said' becomes evaluative commentary on those actions" (p. 157).

Doing Versus Saying

The "doing versus saying" distinction is at the core of linguistic theories of narrative structures. In Ricoeur's (1984) words, "there is no structural analysis of narrative that does not borrow from an explicit or implicit phenomenology of 'doing something'" (p. 56). Genette (1972/1980, pp. 164, 169) distinguishes between narrative of events and narrative of words. For Chatman, narrative "statements are of two kinds—process and stasis—according to whether someone did something or something happened; or whether something simply existed in the story. Process statements are in the mode of DO or HAPPEN . . . Stasis statements are in the mode of IS." (Chatman, 1978, pp. 31–32).[16] In general, a narrative text will comprise a mixture of both purely narrative (action or process) and nonnarrative (descriptive or stasis) clauses. There is never a pure narrative or nonnarrative text. Yet "In modern theories of literature," Bal (1977, p. 89) states, "description occupies a marginal role. The structural analysis of narrative relegates it to a secondary function: It is subordinate to the narration of action." "Description alone is not enough to constitute a narrative; narrative for its part does not exclude description. . . . Description [is] a narrative luxury . . . with an essential ornamental function" (Bal, 1977, pp. 89–90) or with the function of varying narrative tempo, "a suspension of the story or of . . . the 'action'" (Genette, 1972/1980, p. 100).

Stories (or narrative discourses) are a particular kind of action discourse, that is, "discourse which is interpreted as a sequence of actions and their properties" (van Dijk, 1980, p. 13). Not each sentence in an action discourse must necessarily be about action, but most of them are. "Non-story elements may be found in a narrative text just as story elements may be found in a nonnarrative text" (Rimmon-Kenan, 1983, p. 15). In particular, evaluative, descriptive, and expository clauses will often enter into a minimal narrative. The journalist who described the violent events of the fascist attack in Lucca could have spent a few sentences describing the Socialist Youth Club or whether the night of the attacks was a beautiful, early spring night without fundamentally altering the narrative character of the article. In any case, the journalist does spend a few words evaluating the police behavior, "continuing in their zealous and precious job of defending the law equally for everyone, except for the socialists," again without fundamentally altering the narrative character of the article. Narrative texts are those where "the distinctive traits of the narrative genre . . . are quantitatively predominant" (Bal, 1977, p. 13).[17]

Narrative: A Visual Summary

The circles of Figure 2.1 summarize graphically the linguists' and literary critics' arguments on narrative. The larger circle on the left represents all available text genres, of which narrative is only a subset (the smaller inner circle). Within the genre of narrative, description, evaluation, and action (or narrative proper, with its sequences of skeleton narrative sentences) mix in various proportions as shown by the partially overlapping circles on the right (the circles overlap because narrative elements do not necessarily occupy distinct and separate positions in a text; more to the point, both description and evaluation may be part of the linguistic portrayal of narrative action: "terrorist" versus "freedom fighter" or "martyr"; "the man, dressed in poor clothes."). *It is on the larger circle of narrative proper and of human events that we are focusing in this book.* The focus is on what people do, not on what people say, feel, think (although we will also explore ways of dealing with description and, especially, evaluation).

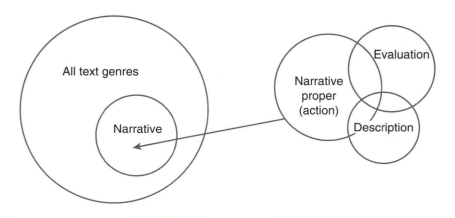

Figure 2.1   The Collocation of Narrative Texts and Narrative Elements

Zooming Into the Narrative Clause

Little by little, we have shifted our focus from such macrostructural characteristics of a text in terms of genre (narrative), sequences, story, and plot to microlevel structures such as the types of characters/actors and verbs (namely, action) that you are more likely to find in narrative texts. Little by little, we have zoomed into the surface representation of narrative as embedded in the structure of language itself, in the clauses and processes. Deep, narrative, macro (semantic) structures map onto surface (syntactic) structures through a subject-noun phrase, a verb phrase, and adverbial elements (for time and space). According to Todorov,[18]

> A narrative grammar is made up of three primary categories: the proper name, the adjective, and the verb . . . Syntactically, the proper name corresponds to the agent. But the agent can be either subject or object . . . The appearance of an object depends upon the transitive or intransitive character of the verb.

Todorov found that syntactic structure in Boccaccio's *Decameron*. Labov also found that structure in the narratives of African Americans living in Harlem (see Labov, 1972, 375 ff.). Narrative clauses, in other words, are characterized by a simple syntactic structure patterned after the canonical form of the language (subject-verb-object structure with some modifiers, such as time and space of verb, but where the verb in narrative is typically an action). Halliday (1985/1994) would later put it this way:

> Language enables human beings to build a mental picture of reality, to make sense of what goes on around them and inside them . . . the clause plays a central role, because it embodies a general principle for modeling experience—namely, the principle that reality is made up of PROCESSES . . . There is a basic difference, that we become aware of at a very early age (three to four months), between inner and outer experience: between what we experience as going on "out there," in the world around us, and what we experience as going on inside ourselves . . . The prototypical form of the "outer" experience is that of actions and events: things happen, and people, or other actors, do things, or make them happen. (p. 106)

Narrative deals predominantly with "the 'outer' experience . . . of actions and events," particularly human actions and human events. For Halliday (1985/1994), both inner and outer experiences are represented linguistically as processes in the clause, where,

> A process consists, in principle, of three components:
>
> (i) the process itself;
>
> (ii) participants in the process; and

(iii) circumstances associated with the process.

In this interpretation of what is going on, there is doing, a doer, and a location where the doing takes place. This tripartite interpretation of processes is what lies behind the grammatical distinction of word classes into verbs, nouns, and the rest. (p. 108)

Participants/Characters

If events are the dominant characteristic of narrative, and events are essentially actions, as captured by verbs, characters occupy a secondary position. It is the action that defines the event, although without characters there can be no action. And if the event is an action, the character is most likely human or has at least anthropomorphic features (from elves to talking horses and magic rings). There is a long tradition in poetics of privileging actions over actors. As Aristotle put it in his *Poetics:*

> Tragedy is a representation not of people as such but of actions and of life and both happiness and unhappiness rest on action . . . [A]nd while men do have certain qualities by virtue of their character, it is in their actions that they achieve, or fail to achieve, happiness . . . [W]ithout action you would not have a tragedy, but one without character would be feasible. (Halliwell, trans., 1987, pp. 37–38)

Propp (1968) similarly wrote,

> The names of the dramatis personae change (as well as the attributes of each), but neither their actions nor functions change . . . The question of *what* a tale's dramatis personae do is an important one for the study of the tale, but the question of *who* does it and *how* it is done already fall within the province of accessory study. (p. 20)

Indeed, the 31 invariant functions that Propp found in Russian folktales are nothing but actions (e.g., the hero's actions). Greimas, in reducing to 5 the number of Propp's functions, proposed to describe and classify narrative characters according to what they do (hence the name *actants*)—once more reproducing the subordination of character to action despite Greimas's (1966) focus on *actants* (see Rimmon-Kenan's (1983, pp. 34–35) excellent brief summary of Greimas's work). And, again, Greimas's functions are essentially actions (nominalized, i.e., verbs turned into nouns), such as the hero's *arrival* (hero arrives), *mission, trial,* and *tasks accomplished.*

Characteristics/Traits

Characters, of course, will have certain characteristics, personal qualities of a character or "traits." These traits are typically, although not exclusively, expressed grammatically as adjectives (Chatman, 1978, p. 125; Todorov, 1969, p. 31). In the absence of explicit character traiting, we can also infer character from action (Rimmon-Kenan, 1983, pp. 60–61; Toolan, 1988, p. 102).

Processes

The process proper is "typically realized by" a verbal group, a participant by a nominal group (typically mapped grammatically onto subjects and complements, depending on the transitivity/intransitivity of the verb— intransitive verbs have no complement), and a circumstance by an adverbial group or prepositional phrase (Halliday, 1985/1994, p. 109). For Halliday, processes group into three main classes:

1. doing (or material), further divided into
   (a) happening (being created)
   (b) creating, changing
   (c) doing (to), acting

2. sensing (or mental), further divided into
   (a) seeing
   (b) feeling
   (c) thinking

3. being (or relational), further divided into
   (a) symbolizing
   (b) having identity
   (c) having attribute

In addition, there are three more subclasses of secondary processes,

1. behavioral,
2. verbal, and
3. existential,

located at the boundaries between different combinations of primary processes, "sharing some features of each, and thus acquiring a character of their own" (Halliday, 1994: 107): behavioral between material and mental, verbal between mental and relational, and existential between relational and material. In this classificatory scheme of processes, narrative is mostly made up of material processes, particularly doing (to)/acting with some verbal and behavioral processes.

Circumstances

For Halliday (1985/1994), the circumstances of a process refer to "the location of an event in time or space, its manner, or its cause" (p. 150). They refer to notions such as "when, where, how and why" something happens (p. 150). "Whereas participants function in the mood grammar as Subject or Complement, circumstances map into Adjuncts . . . They are typically expressed not as nominal groups but as either adverbial groups or prepositional phrases" (p. 150). Ricoeur (1984) similarly writes that "the very term 'action,' taken in the narrow sense of what someone does, gets its distinct meaning from its capacity for being used in conjunction with other terms of the whole network" (pp. 54–55), a "conceptual network," made up of actors, actions, goals, motives, agents, circumstances, and outcomes. According to Ricoeur, "these terms or others akin to them occur in our answers to questions that can be classified as questions about 'what,' 'why,' 'who,' 'how,' 'with whom,' or 'against whom' in regard to any action" (pp. 54–55). Kenneth Burke (1945/1969), in his *Grammar of Motives*, similarly pays tribute to that simple structure of narrative, to "the five key terms of dramatism," the "pentad of key terms": Act, Scene, Agent, Agency, Purpose—"what was done (act), when and where it was done (scene), who did it (agent), how he did it (agency), and why (purpose)" (p. xv). Todorov (1968/1981) referred to this simple structure as "grammar of stories" and so did Prince (1973) in his work on stories. But it was in the work of cognitive psychologists that the label *story grammar* would become popular (on this point, see Franzosi, 2004b, p. 347, note 44).

A Story Grammar for Sociohistorical Research

We can define a "story grammar" as the set of rules that provides the categories into which the various invariant elements of a story fall (e.g., actor, action, time, space), the nature of each category (e.g., a text, a number, a date; allowed to occur one or multiple times), and their reciprocal relationships (van Dijk, 1972, p. 145; see also Rumelhart, 1975, p. 213). Borrowing from transformational syntax the concept of "rewrite rule" (also called *production*, and notationally expressed by a right-pointing arrow →), where an element to the left of the rule is "rewritten" in terms of its constituent elements, to the right of the rule, we can rewrite the narrative clause in terms of subject-action-object,

<narrative clause>   →   {<subject>} {<action>} [{<object>}]

or in terms of Halliday's participant-process-participant language,

<narrative clause>   →   {<participant>} {<process>} [{<participant>}]

where the symbols used in rewrite rules have the following meaning (see Table 2.2):

Table 2.2   The Symbols of Rewrite Rules[a]

< >	angular brackets denote an element that can be further rewritten (an element that cannot be further rewritten is called a terminal element and corresponds to the words found in a dictionary, calendar dates and times, or numbers)
→	right-pointing arrow refers to the rewrite rule (or production)
{ }	curly brackets denote elements that can occur more than one time
[ ]	square brackets denote optional elements (they can occur zero or one or more times, depending on the presence of curly brackets)
|	the symbol is equivalent to "or" (as opposed to "and")

a. van Dijk (1972, p. 145), in his work on text grammars (as opposed to the more specific narrative or story grammars), proposed to express a text, T, in terms of the microstructures of the 5 Ws of journalism (who, what, when, where, why, and how) via a similar formal representation.

In my own work, I have referred to the skeleton narrative clause as a "semantic triplet" because it is made up of three elements endowed with meaning. Both the <object> and the second <participant> are enclosed in square brackets, [ ], because their presence is optional. The expression "fascists beat up two workers" has a subject, "fascists," an action, "beat up," and an object, "two workers"; the expression "workers strike" has no object, according to the transitivity/intransitivity of the verb.

This simple, horizontal, relational structure can be aggregated, vertically, into a hierarchical structure with a set of semantic triplets making up an event and a set of events making up a dispute (or macro-event, campaign, story) (Figure 2.2):

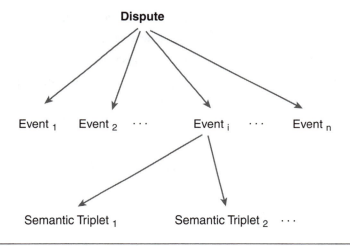

Figure 2.2   Hierarchical Structure of a Story Grammar

With the use of rewrite rules, this structure can be rendered as

<dispute>	→	{<event>} {<document>}
<event>	→	{<semantic triplet>}
<semantic triplet>	→	{<subject>} {<action>} [{<object>}]

The <dispute> represents the initial symbol of the grammar. It is made up of events and cross-referenced to a set of documents.[19] Subjects, actions, and objects (or participants and processes) can be rewritten further to capture substantively relevant attributes of actors and actions.

A subject can be further rewritten as an institution, an individual, or a set of individuals. Of individuals we would like to know the name, occupation, marital status, age, and sex, along with, perhaps, their organizational affiliation (company they work for, political party, trade union). Institutions operate in different societal spheres (religious, political, social, or economic); economic organizations operate in different sectors (chemicals, textiles, banking, etc.), at different levels of aggregation (e.g., shop, plant, firm). Using the rewrite rules and the familiar symbols, we can translate the foregoing discussion into the following formalized structure:

<participant>	→	{<actor>}
<actor>	→	<individual> | <set of individuals> |
		<institution>
<individual>	→	<name of individual>

		[<first name and last name>]
		[<characteristics>]
<name of individual>	→	mayor | president | worker | . . .
<characteristics>	→	[<gender>] [<age>] [<residence>]
		[<nationality>] [<type >] [<occupation>]
		[<work organization>]
		[<trade union affiliation>]
		[<party affiliation>] . . .

. . .

<type>	→	skilled | unskilled | immigrant . . .
<organization>	→	. . . farm worker, industrial worker, technician, manager . . .

. . .

<set of individuals>	→	<name of set> <characteristics>
<name of set>	→	workers | crowd | . . .

. . .

As for the <action> or <process>, there are several items of information of interest. First, an action occurs in time and space, the fundamental categories of narrative. There is no story without time. Narrative time has three aspects, order, duration, and frequency, dealing with three different questions: When? For how long? And how often?[20,21] In comparison, the narrative category of space occupies a less central role in narrative theory since you can still have a story without space (but you cannot without time). An action also has a reason and an outcome. For example, a "strike" could occur over "contract renewal" and result in "10% wage increase" or "one extra paid vacation day." That same strike action can be of several different types: "general," "wildcat," "sit-in," or "to rule." The action may be based on different instruments. Thus, the police might attack a crowd using "batons," "tear gas," and so on. A crowd, in turn, might use "rocks," "sticks," or "Molotov bombs." Finally, there may be a need to relate actions to objects through the case to eliminate semantic ambiguity. There is no ambiguity in understanding the semantic triplet <subject> trade unions <process> organize strike <object> workers (<organization> Ford) even if the specification of the case is missing (trade unions organize a strike *of* Ford workers); but the triplet <subject> workers (<organization> Pirelli) <process> collect signatures <object> workers (<organization> Breda) is semantically ambiguous as it is unclear whether signatures are collected on behalf of or among Breda workers. Explicit links (<case>) can thus be specified to connect actions to objects (e.g., "for," "from," and "to"). In conclusion, the nonterminal symbol <process> may be rewritten as follows:

<process>	→	<verb> [<negation>] [<modality>] <circumstances>
<verb>	→	strike | rally | layoff | charge | . . .
<negation>	→	not
<modality>	→	can | could | may | might | will | . . .
<circumstances >	→	<time> <space> [<type>] [<reason>] [<instrument>] [<outcome>]
<reason>	→	wage increases | layoffs | . . .
<instrument>	→	bomb | gun | . . .
<outcome>	→	positive | negative | disruption | . . .

For <time>, the grammar should specify whether it is a date and/or a time of day, expressed in definite form (June 11, 1949, or 10:15 p.m.) or indefinite form (several days ago; in the morning). For <space>, the grammar should specify whether the geographical location is a territory (with names and levels that vary widely, from state to county, shire, province, departments) or a city (with neighborhoods, streets, and squares). Space can be static (in, at) or dynamic (from, to).

Finally, the grammar rewrites the <object> (the <participant> as complement) as either an actor (i.e., a human agent) or an inanimate noun (e.g., factory, road). This way, expressions such as "workers occupy the factory," "protesters set fire to cars," and so on can easily be expressed in the grammar.

<object>	→	<actor> | <physical object>
<physical object>	→	factory | road | car | . . .

Some of the objects in a story grammar are invariant with respect to the type of narrative analyzed (e.g., <participant> and <process>, <time> and <space>); others may be specific to specific types of narrative. For example, you will find modifiers such as <trade union> in a narrative of strikes; but it is unlikely that, in these narratives, you will find references to personal physical attributes, such as the color of hair, eyes, and so on, much more typical of folktales or fictional narrative. In a story grammar, you can specify any number of modifiers without altering its fundamental structure and tailor the grammar to your specific needs.

Simple Examples of Coding

To understand how a story grammar works in practice, let's code the following simple sentence: "The crowd killed the man." Within the categories of a simple story grammar, the sentence would be coded as (Participant: (Actor: *crowd*)) (Process: (Verb: *killed*)) (Participant: (Object: (Actor: *man*))). Similarly, the sentence "a crowd of 50 men killed a 56-year-old man" would yield the following code: (Participant: (Actor: *crowd*) (Characteristics: (Number: *50*) (Sex: *male*))) (Process: (Verb: *killed*)) (Participant: (Object: (Actor: *man*) (Characteristics: (Age: *56*)))). The sentence can be preceded and followed by other skeleton narrative sentences to provide a fuller narrative, as in "In Macon, Georgia, a crowd of 50 men killed today a 56-year-old man who had outraged a young girl. The police did not make any arrest." to yield the following set of chronologically ordered semantic triplets:

Semantic triplet 1: (Participant: (Actor: *man*) (Characteristics: (Age: *56*))) (Process: (Verb: *outrages*)) (Participant: (Object: (Actor: *girl*) (Characteristics: (Age: *young*)))

Semantic triplet 2: (Participant: (Actor: *crowd*) (Characteristics: (Number: *50*) (Sex: *male*))) (Process: (Verb: *killed*)) (Circumstances: (Time: (Date: (Indefinite date: *today*))) (Space: (City: Macon (State: *Georgia*))))) (Participant: (Object: (Actor: *man*) (Characteristics: (Age: *56*))))

Semantic triplet 3: (Participant: (Actor: *police*)) (Process: (Negation: *not*) (Verb: *make arrest*))

A More Complex Example

To appreciate the full power of a story grammar as an organizational structure for narrative information, let's look at a more complex story. Let's go back to the *Avanti!* (1921) newspaper article that we saw in the opening chapter of this book, reproduced here in full for convenience.

Lucca's Labor Chamber Destroyed. Last night, around 10 pm, a group of fascists, crossing the city walls that lead from the fortress of San Martino to that of San Paolino, where the Labor Chamber is located, knocked down the entrance door and the internal side ones, breaking all the furniture and removing documents and red flags, and a poster with "Labor Chamber" written on it. Then, the fascists went to the headquarters of the Socialist Youth Club, located in via Boccherini. Unable to get in through the main door, they tore down a wall and once inside they destroyed all the furniture and various portraits, and removed all the documents. Some gunshots were fired in the air. Heading for the Railway Workers' Union, the fascists found it guarded by police, and unable to get in, they went to the custodian's home (who didn't answer). Police, continuing in their zealous and precious job of defending the law equally for everyone, except for the socialists, arrested some fifteen socialists belonging to the Workers' Leagues and unsympathetic to Fascism. Talking about justice! (p. 21)

Let's focus on the first sentence of this story:

Last night, around 10 pm, a group of fascists, crossing the city walls that lead from the fortress of San Martino to that of San Paolino, where the Labor Chamber is located, knocked down the entrance door and the internal side ones, breaking all the furniture and removing documents and red flags, and a poster with 'Labor Chamber' written on it. (p. 21)

The sentence is a good example of narrative text, made up of clauses characterized mostly by Halliday's processes of doing, with minimal description ("the city walls that lead from the fortress of San Martino to that of San Paolino, where the Labor Chamber is located") and no evaluation (indeed, in the entire article, description and evaluation are minimal, with evaluation relegated to the ironic reference to police behavior at the end of the article). When each of the constitutive clauses of this long sentence is assigned sentence status,[22] the narrative would look something like this:

1. Last night, around 10 p.m., a group of fascists crossed the city walls toward the Labor Chamber.
2. The walls lead from the fortress of San Martino to that of San Paolino.
3. The Labor Chamber is located there.
4. The fascists knocked down the entrance door and the internal side ones.
5. They broke all the furniture.
6. They removed documents and red flags, and a poster with "Labor Chamber" written on it.

Of these six new sentences, two are descriptive sentences (sentences 2 and 3), that is, sentences where there are no social actors doing something. The other four sentences (1, 4, 5, and 6) are typical "skeleton narrative sentences," that is, temporally ordered sentences where some actors perform some actions. These six sentences (together with the article lead) give us the event ("destruction of Lucca's Labor Chamber"), the event time and place ("last night, around 10 pm" in the city of "Lucca" and, within the city, "the city walls," "fortress of San Martino," "fortress of San Paolino"), the actors involved ("fascists"), their number ("a group"), the actors' actions ("crossed," denoting movement, and "knock down," "break," "remove," denoting violence), and the explicit targets of their actions ("Labor Chamber" and, more specifically, "entrance door," "internal side doors," "furniture," documents," "red flags," "poster") but also the actors' implicit targets of the fascists' actions ("the Socialists" of the Labor Chamber).

Within the categories of a simplified story grammar, this information can be structured as follows:

Semantic triplet 1: (Participant: (Actor: *fascists*) (Characteristics: (Number: *group*))) (Process: (Verb: *go*) (Circumstances: (Time: (Date: 03/31/1921) (Hour: 10 pm))) (Space: (City: *Lucca*) ((Space direction: *through*) (Location within city: *city walls*)) ((Space direction: *from*) (Location within city: *San Martino fortress*)) ((Space direction: *to*) (Location within city: (Building: *Labor Chamber* (Location: *San Paolino fortress*)))))))

Semantic triplet 2: (Participant: (Actor: *fascists*) (Characteristics: (Number: *group*))) (Process: (Verb: *knock down*)) (Participant: (Object: (Physical object: (Building: Labor Chamber (Location: *San Paolino fortress*)) (Part of object: *entrance door*) (Part of object: *internal side doors*))))

Semantic triplet 3: (Participant: (Actor: *fascists*) (Characteristics: (Number: *group*))) (Process: (Verb: *break*)) (Participant: (Object: (Physical object: *furniture*)) (Characteristics: (Number: *all*))

Semantic triplet 4: (Participant: (Actor: *fascists*) (Characteristics: (Number: *group*))) (Process: (Verb: *remove*)) (Participant: (Object: (Physical object: *documents*) (Physical object: *red flags*) (Physical object: *poster*)))

The example shows that, by and large, most narrative elements found in the original input text also appear in the output. The grammar does provide a tool for structuring narrative in ways such that the individual textual elements of the original narrative find appropriate pigeonholes for their classification in the grammar. However, it is also important to note that the process of narrative coding has involved some manipulation of the original text, however minimal: forming sentences out of clauses, dropping descriptive clauses from the coding, and incorporating important elements of these clauses into the <circumstances> of coded narrative clauses, notably <space>, and even rewording the language of some clauses (e.g., clauses 1 through 3 as rendered in <semantic triplet> 1).

When coded within the categories of a story grammar, the rest of the newspaper article from *Avanti!* would look something like this:

Semantic triplet 5: (Participant: (Actor: *fascists*) (Characteristics: (Number: *group*))) (Process: (Verb: *go to*) (Circumstances: (Space: (City: *Lucca*) (Location: *Via Boccherini*) (Building: *Socialist Youth Club*))))

Semantic triplet 6: (Participant: (Actor: *fascists*) (Characteristics: (Number: *group*))) (Process: (Negation: *not*) (Modality: *can*) (Verb: *get in*))

Semantic triplet 7: (Participant: (Actor: *fascists*) (Characteristics: (Number: *group*))) (Process: (Verb: *tear down*)) (Participant: (Object: (Physical object: *Socialist Youth Club*) (Part of Object: *wall*)))

Semantic triplet 8: (Participant: (Actor: *fascists*) (Characteristics: (Number: *group*))) (Process: (Verb: *destroy*)) (Participant: (Object: (Physical object: *furniture*) (Characteristics: (Number: *all*))) (Object: (Physical object: *portrait*) (Characteristics: (Number: *various*)))))

Semantic triplet 9: (Participant: (Actor: *fascists*) (Characteristics: (Number: *group*))) (Process: (Verb: *remove*)) (Participant: (Object: (Physical object: *documents*)) (Characteristics: (Number: *all*)))

Semantic triplet 10: (Participant: (Actor: *?*)) (Process: (Verb: *fire*) (Circumstances: (Instrument: *gun*)))

Semantic triplet 11: (Participant: (Actor: *fascists*) (Characteristics: (Number: *group*))) (Process: (Verb: *go to*) (Circumstances: (Space: (City: *Lucca*) (Building: *Railway Workers' Union*))))

Semantic triplet 12: (Participant: (Actor: *police*)) (Process: (Verb: *guard*)) (Participant: (Object: (Physical object: (Building: *Railway Workers' Union*))))

Semantic triplet 13: (Participant: (Actor: *fascists*) (Characteristics: (Number: *group*))) (Process: (Negation: *not*) (Modality: *can*) (verb: *get in*))

Semantic triplet 14: (Participant: (Actor: *fascists*) (Characteristics: (Number: *group*))) (Process: (Verb: *go to*) (Circumstances: (Space: *home* (Ownership: Actor: *custodian*))))

Semantic triplet 15: (Participant: (Actor: *custodian*)) (Process: (Negation: *not*) (Verb: *answer*))

Semantic triplet 16: (Participant: (Actor: *police*)) (Process: (Verb: *arrest*)) (Participant: (Object: (Actor: (*Socialists*)) (Characteristics: (Number: 15) (Union affiliation: *Workers' Leagues*)))))

So What? (A Story Point of My Own)

No doubt, there is a very close relationship between input and output: The output has preserved much of the original information in its narrative format. A simple comparison of coded output against text input will reveal that characteristic. Yet, you may wonder, why bother? What is the point of building such a complicated machinery to get, in the end, what is nearly the same of what we had to start with? A classic case of much ado about nothing!

Why should it matter that most narrative elements found in the original input text also appear in the coded output but appropriately organized in the coding categories of a complex story grammar? It matters because

1. for each category, you know exactly what it contains (e.g., an actor, a reason, a city); thus, you know where to look if you are interested in actors;

2. within each coding category, you find one, and only one, textual element (e.g., the specific actor "workers" or "police");

3. for each textual element, you also know its exact relation to other textual elements (e.g., an actor related to a specific reason for a specific action; e.g., "workers" "strike");

4. in this simplified and reorganized format, textual data are ready for quantitative analysis.

Of Narrative Elements and Limits to QNA

On the *Atlanta Daily World* of April 29, 1936 (evidence added to highlight evaluation), we read:

> GEORGIA ADDS ANOTHER LYNCHING. *FURTHER evidence of the urgent need of an effective anti-lynching law was shown* yesterday morning when a mob of fifty white Georgians took Lint Shaw, 45, a sharecropper, from the jail at Royston and lynched him a few hours before his trial was to be held. A rope was tied around the waist of the victim's body which was suspended from a tree and riddled with bullets . . . Shaw was charged with attempted assault on a white woman . . . *[W]e are not attempting to judge the merits or demerits of this case because we feel this is the duty of the courts. But we are saying we unequivocably oppose lynching. This evil is a menace to the foundation of our government. If the states don't stop lynching, the federal government should, and we feel eventually will. The Atlanta World has always stood for law and order. Every man is entitled to a speedy and fair trial and we oppose to people taking the law into their own hands at their will. It is our hope that the day will soon come when law and order will prevail here in Georgia at all times. Lynching is a blot on civilization and it is an insult to constituted authority. Let us help stop lynching and make our country safe for democracy.* (p. 6, column 1)

In this news article, the narrative element of evaluation (highlighted in the excerpt by the use of italics) is dominant compared with action or narrative proper. Another article in the same day for the same paper (p. 1, column 7) provides a brief description of Lint Shaw's wife: "Mrs. Georgia Shaw, a brown skinned woman with coal black hair and Indian features, who speaks only when spoken to."

Different types of narrative will use a different mix of action, evaluation, and description, depending on the rhetorical strategies of the writer/teller. The story grammar developed here, with its participants as social actors and processes as actions, cannot cope well with the linguistic characteristics of evaluation and description: Participants and processes of these narrative elements are typically not in the form of social actors and actions (see Halliday, 1985/1994, pp. 106–144, for various types of participants and processes).

Attempting to code descriptive and evaluative elements of narrative (or nonnarrative texts altogether) in the categories of a story grammar is likely to result in poor-quality coded output. Cognitive psychologists have argued that "distortions in recall (and understanding of a story) will occur at points where ambiguity or violation of an ideal structure occurs in the surface structure" (Mandler & Johnson, 1977, p. 134). We can expect that same distortion in coding when the surface structure of a narrative (in its descriptive and evaluative parts) does not match the ideal narrative structure of the story grammar coding scheme. In other words, the further the distance between the structure of a story grammar and the surface structure of the story being coded (as in description and evaluation), the greater likelihood we can expect of coding errors and/or intercoder differences (leading to lower reliability).

What Social Scientists Have to
Say About Texts: Content Analysis

While linguists and literary critics, under the influence of structuralism, were busy trying to uncover the invariant structures of narratives, social scientists got busy with a project of their own involving texts. But while the first remained firmly anchored to the words—as, no doubt, fit for linguists—social scientists approached those same words with the idea of turning them into numbers. Their aim was to quantify the information encoded in messages with a technique they named *content analysis* (for a collection of the main methodological and substantive contributions in this tradition, see Franzosi, 2008). Precursors aside, we can safely date the origins of the technique to the 1940s, to the early years of the Second World War and the work of Harold D. Lasswell. During the war, as director of the Experimental Division for the Study of War Time Communications in Washington, D.C., Lasswell's goals and those of his associates were to develop "a research technique for the objective, systematic, and quantitative description of the manifest content of communication" (Berelson, 1952, p. 18; for this history, see Franzosi, 2008, pp. xxiii–xxiv). And the way he was proposing to do it was through a coding scheme, made up of a set of coding categories (namely, topics or themes found in the text) that when uniformly applied by coders to a set of texts would yield quantitative measures of the semantics of these texts (on these issues, see Franzosi, 2008, pp. xxiv–xxv).

The Coding Scheme

Questions

Where do content analysis coding schemes come from? How are they designed? Are they based on the investigator's research interests or on invariant properties of texts (like story grammars)? Do they change for every project, like the questions of a questionnaire in survey research, or are they stable across projects?

Answers

In Lasswell's mind, coding schemes were supposed to be theoretically constructed. "Since by means of content analysis we provide data for a science of politics, our observations must be related to a systematic body of postulates, definitions, rules, hypotheses and laws" (Lasswell, 1942, p. 3). Coding schemes should be derived from a systematic theory of politics. They should allow investigators to test specific hypotheses about that theory. "One sound rule of choice (in coding categories) is to classify with a view of obtaining data which are relevant to definite hypotheses . . . " (Lasswell, 1938, p. 198). In reality, content analysis schemes have been typically derived (inductively) in an interactive process between an investigator's initial research interests, careful reading of specific texts that address these research interests, design of preliminary coding categories (and where coding schemes available from past research play a fundamental role), coding of texts into these categories, and refining the categories till the investigator feels that the coding scheme adequately captures what is said in the selected texts in light of the investigator's specific research needs. Ironically, qualitative researchers recommend the same approach—without counting in the end.

QNA and Content Analysis: Spelling Out the Differences

Questions

Story grammars, rewrite rules, narrative . . . Aren't you (Roberto Franzosi) just proposing content analysis under different labels? Where is the difference? Isn't what you call a story grammar just another coding scheme, your elements of the grammar just coding categories? Since there is a long scholarly tradition in the social sciences in the methodology of content analysis going as far back as the 1940s, if not earlier, why do you feel compelled to invent new labels?

Answer

True. A story grammar is nothing but a coding scheme and each constituent element of the grammar nothing but a coding category in the language of content analysis—and you can certainly use that language if you wish. Beyond that, however, there are *fundamental* differences between story grammar and content analysis approaches to text. Let me highlight the main differences.

1. The categories of a grammar are functional, linguistic based. They reflect properties of the text itself (and in particular of a specific type of text, narrative). In content analysis, categories are constructed on the basis of the researchers' substantive and theoretical interests. They reflect what the researcher wants to get out of a text with reference to specific research questions.

2. Coding categories in a grammar are formally and explicitly related to one another throughout the coding scheme via a set of rewrite rules (e.g., subjects are linked to actions, actions to objects, and subjects, actions, and objects are linked to their modifiers). No such formal relation exists between content analysis coding categories. They are typically listed seriatim (or, at most, grouped together under broader headings).

3. Rewrite rules generate an event (or a larger macro-event, such as the dispute) in terms of nonterminal and terminal symbols. The set of all terminal symbols constitutes the lexicon found in the text.

   a. Coding text in terms of terminal symbols within explicitly linked linguistic categories gives coded output the flavor of a natural language narrative, with coded output organized in chronologically ordered sentencelike structures and with very little original "narrative" information lost in the process of coding.[23]

   b. The narrative richness of the information coded in a story grammar, in ways that closely resemble the original narrative, *delivers data that are more nearly hypothesis free than with traditional content analysis* (since data are collected through a coding scheme that is independent of any particular theoretical concern but reflect the very structure of narrative). This property makes secondary data analysis easier. In content analysis, categories designed for specific theoretical questions are unlikely to suit researchers with different questions—and that is true even for the original researchers who wish to ask different questions of their data (Markoff, Shapiro, & Weitman, 1975, p. 41).

   c. The wealth of available information should also allow rich and fine-grained analyses, the empirical testing of hitherto untested and untestable propositions.

4. In content analysis, coders play a greater role in the coding process than in a story grammar approach. How deeply the two approaches differ can be seen from Holsti's definition of coding, in one of the earliest textbooks on content analysis, as "the process whereby raw data are systematically transformed and *aggregated* [italics added] into units which permit precise description of relevant content characteristics" (Holsti, 1969, p. 94). Coding, in content analysis, assigns text to *aggregated* categories, typically theoretically defined. Data coding and data aggregation go hand in hand, the coder performing both tasks. In a story grammar approach to coding, coding consists of assigning parts of text to the natural and familiar categories of a story: who was involved, what they did, when, and where. Coders are not involved in theoretical decisions during the coding process (e.g., whether a demand of "10% wage increase" is a material or postmaterial demand) (see also Tilly, 1995, p. 395). This decision, if necessary, is made at a later stage by the researchers themselves. Coders keep close to the text, in terms of both narrative structures and lexicon. In content analysis, however much researchers may try to reduce coders' discretion in fitting text into abstract categories through written coding rules, the abstract coding categories invariably result in the contamination of the measurement instrument.[24] Coders play "surrogate scientist."[25]

Hypothesis-Free Data? Limits to a Claim

Question

How can you claim that quantitative narrative analysis produces hypothesis-free data and at the same time write the following:

1. Specific modifiers (attributes) of a story grammar may change with different applications (e.g., the actor modifier <trade union>, which may be relevant in a project on strikes but not, perhaps, in children's stories, or personal physical attributes, such as the color of hair and eyes, typically not given in a narrative of strikes but typical of folktales or fictional narrative)?

2. A story grammar works well with narrative type texts only; furthermore, even with this broad class of texts, it works well only with narrative proper but not with description and evaluation (also typically part of narrative).

   How can a structure like a story grammar can be "invariant" and yet change depending on the research projects? And if it changes with the research projects, then, it is tied to specific questions and hypotheses, hardly a hypothesis-free scenario.

Answer

I am not new to that claim. In my first article on quantitative narrative analysis, published in 1989, I wrote (Franzosi, 1989, pp. 263; also pp. 289, 294) that a story grammar approach to content analysis "makes the process of data collection independent of any prior specification of hypotheses, because virtually all relevant information provided by the sources can be easily coded." In that form or another ("nearly hypothesis free" or "more hypothesis free"), I repeated that claim across a number of subsequent publications. Perhaps this needs to be qualified.

First, a fully specified grammar would contain all necessary character traiting (the psychological or physical attributes of an individual, such as race or eye color, or the institutional affiliation of an individual or group, including trade unions). In some texts, some traits may never be mentioned (e.g., the color of eyes in strike narratives). It is simply a matter of convenience to streamline a story grammar used in a specific project to avoid the clutter of categories, which would always be empty. The full story grammar is still invariant; for ease of data entry, some categories may be eliminated.

Second, no data, of course, are ever hypothesis free. The simple choice of collecting some data as opposed to others, of looking one way for explanations and evidence rather than others, implies ways of seeing, selection criteria, hunches, *hypotheses.* Selecting to focus on narratives, rather than variables, as a way to study sociohistorical reality implies the hypothesis that actors and their actions are key to explanations in the human sciences (the idea of going "in search of the actor," as I have put it; Franzosi, 2004b, pp. 3–4). Within narrative, selecting to focus on narrative proper rather than description and evaluation implies the hypothesis that doing and action are more relevant than saying and discourse for those explanations. The irony with which the *Avanti!* newspaper article leaves the reader ("talking about justice!") is gone from the coded version of that same story.

My claim is narrower: *When compared with content analysis,* with its theoretically driven and abstract coding categories, quantitative narrative analysis and its story grammar provide a research tool that delivers data less tied to a specific theoretical framework *at least in the process of measurement of actors and their actions.*

Interview Data and Narrative

In the 1930s and 1940s, while Harold D. Lasswell, professor of political science at Chicago, was developing content analysis, Paul Lazarsfeld, a sociologist from Columbia, was busy developing his version of a quantitative methodology for the social sciences: survey research. There are many similarities between the two techniques: They both rely on a set of categories as the instrument of measurement (the coding scheme in content analysis and the questionnaire in survey research), and they both rely on a human being (the coder and the interviewer) to administer this instrument to a set of texts (content analysis) or of interviewees (survey research) (Franzosi, 2008, p. xl).

And, of course, they are both quantitative: They deal with words and turn them into numbers. They do so by ticking off preset items in a list (a coding category in content analysis and a closed-ended question in survey research, where a closed-ended question is one that admits only preassigned responses[26], in contrast with an open-ended question, to which respondents are free to answer in their own words); then, they both count the ticks to get the numbers. In their drive to achieve scientific status, both content analysis and survey research foregrounded issues of methods and technical language (e.g., objectivity, reliability, sampling) and backgrounded issues of meaning and interpretation (e.g., the role of coders and interviewers) (Franzosi, 2008, pp. xxiv–xxvii).

Large-scale survey research, with its thousands of respondents, can ill afford open-ended questions—answers to these questions, to be quantified, need to be recoded, using content analysis, for themes (what respondents say in their answers) and sentiments (how they feel about certain topics, people, institutions, objects, or places). But other social science approaches, based on much smaller numbers of respondents and on a more qualitative approach to data gathering, heavily rely on open-ended questions to elicit responses from interviewees.

Qualitative scholars do not analyze quantitatively the textual data that comes from people's written and oral words and/or the observer's own notes. Rather, in the presentation of their findings, qualitative scholars use snippets of actors' responses, in the actors' own words, as evidence of themes emerging from the data, simply, or of theoretical points drawn from the transcripts of their oral texts. As Taylor and Bogdan (1984) recommend,

> *Ground your writing in specific examples.* Qualitative research yields rich descriptions. Illustrative quotations and descriptions convey a deep understanding of what settings and people are like and provide evidence that things are the way you report them to be. Your research report should be filled with clear examples. These should be short and to the point, however. Most readers find it tedious to read through long quotes. You should resist the temptation to overuse colorful data. (pp. 153–154)

Not all responses to open-ended questions contain stories, but often they do. As Mishler (1986) remarked, in one of the early attempts to explore the relationship between narrative and survey research and interviewing, "Telling stories is far from unusual in everyday conversation and it is apparently no more unusual for interviewees to respond to questions with narratives if they are given some room to speak" (p. 69). Indeed, as Mishler goes on to note (pp. 69–72), an interviewee may respond with a story even to closed-ended questions (although, to know that story, we would need the complicity of a zealous interviewer who writes it down). Thus, you will find narratives and stories in responses to in-depth open-ended interviews, focus groups, and, especially, oral history and personal narratives.[27] Narratives are part and parcel of any anthropological and sociological fieldwork.[28]

The narratives embedded in responses to open-ended questions take different forms. Sometimes, they refer to specific events, as in the story told Becker (1963) by a marijuana user:

> We didn't know where to get any [marijuana]. None of us knew where to get it or how to find out where to get it. Well, there was this one chick there . . . she had some spade [Negro] friends and she had turned on before with them. Maybe once or twice. But she knew a little more about it than any of the rest of us. So she got hold of some, through these spade friends, and one night she brought down a couple of sticks. (pp. 62–63)

At other times, the narratives refer to ongoing processes, rather than specific events, as in the response a female "professor at a northern university" gave Feagin and Sikes (1994) in an interview about racial attitudes:

> Both of our sons went to high school here in this city, and everybody, every other parent in the school, always assumed that our children had full scholarships. And they didn't. My husband and I struggled and paid their tuition, you know. But they assumed, because they were black, that they had full scholarships. (p. 87)

And interview narratives, whether of specific events or of ongoing processes, and no different from newspaper narratives or any other narratives, often include evaluation, as put to DeVault (1991) by one of the women in her study of the gendered nature of work in the home.

> My son and I use diet margarine . . . And then one of my daughters who's a vegetarian and is so concerned about what he eats—she's very concerned about fiber and roughage—he uses straight butter, and she wants to have it in the house when she comes, but she doesn't use a lot of it. And my husband wants everything to be polyunsaturated. So I have to read all the labels. But then he wants to have cream in his coffee, *so what's the use? What's the use, if you are going to keep having beef* [italics added]? (pp. 223–224)

Or, more rarely, description, as in the words of the volunteer described in McAdam's (1988) *Freedom Summer*:

> Canvassing is very trying, you walk a little dusty street, with incredibly broken down shacks. The people sitting on porches staring away into nowhere—the

sweat running down your face! Little kids half-naked in raggy clothes all over the place—this is what you face with your little packet of "Freedom Forms" . . . you walk up to a porch, knock on a door and enter into another world. . . . The walls are inevitably covered with a funeral hall calendar, a portrait calendar of President Kennedy, old graduation pictures. Maybe a new cheap lamp from Fred's dollar store. (p. 78)

And even such simple description contains evaluation. To the extent that the purpose of qualitative data analysis is that of "developing an in-depth understanding of the settings or people under study," these snippets of conversations provide valuable insights into the respondents' world (Taylor & Bogdan, 1984, p. 129). Numbers would certainly not reach the same depth. But even in qualitative research, data analysis, through simple tools ("tables of data; tally sheets of themes; summaries or proportions of various statements, phrases, or terms; and similarly reduced and transformed groupings of data"), aims to "assist the researcher in understanding and observing certain *patterns in the data* [italics added]" (Berg, 2004, p. 39). *That being the goal, the more sophisticated tools of organization and analysis of textual data, narrative data in particular, proposed in this book could certainly help qualitative researchers in this task of drawing patterns out of data, without breaching some of the more fundamental epistemological premises that separate them from quantitative researchers* (e.g., the division between subject and object, the research processes starting from the ground up, from data to theory, rather than top down, from hypotheses).

To capture more closely the complex worldview often expressed in open-ended interviews, a story grammar would have to be expanded, beyond the <semantic triplet> centered on actors and their actions, to include both description and evaluation. Both evaluation and description would be optional elements of a story and could be attached to any object contemplated in a story grammar, in particular, events, actors, or physical objects:

<event>   →   {<semantic triplet>} [{<evaluation>}]

                        [{<description>}]

. . .

<participant>   →   {<actor>} [{<evaluation>}] [{<description>}]

. . .

<evaluation>   →   negative | positive | neutral

Such an approach to QNA that encompasses not only action but also description and evaluation would closely resemble Roberts's (1989, 1997) linguistic approach to content analysis. For Roberts, a text—any text and not just narrative—can be analyzed via a generic semantic grammar, based on four functional forms: perception, recognition, justification, and evaluation.

> Perceptions *describe processes* (or sequences of events) that take place over time . . . Recognitions *describe states of affairs* . . . justifications are . . . intended to *judge* the rightness or wrongness of *a process*. Evaluations are . . . intended . . . to *judge* the goodness or badness of *a state of affairs* . . . (Roberts, 1989, pp. 154–155)

Thus, for narrative texts, perceptions (as processes and events) provide the core elements of narrative (i.e., action), whereas recognitions describe and justifications and evaluations evaluate.

What Social Scientists Have to Say About Narrative

Over the past two decades, not just linguists and literary critics but social scientists as well, in particular sociologists, have paid increasing attention to the study of narrative. Sociologists have privileged traditional, qualitative approaches to narrative (e.g., Kohler Riessman, 1993). But they have also attempted to exploit the invariant properties of narrative (e.g., the five Ws structure of Who, What, When, Where, Why, and How; or the sequentially ordered nature of narrative discourse) to introduce more formal method-ological approaches to narrative.

The work of Abell (1987, 1993), Carley (1993), Fararo and Skvoretz (1986; Fararo, 1993; Skvoretz, 1993; Skvoretz & Fararo, 1989) stand out as the most formalized social science approaches to narrative (or texts in general). Although drawing from different disciplinary backgrounds—Abell from rational choice theory and Carley and Fararo and Skvoretz from cognitive psychology and artificial intelligence—these authors pro-vide formal representations of social action (actors doing something pro or against other actors) based on rewrite rules.

For Abell, a narrative is made up of actors performing some actions (that are at least partially ordered in time). Using set theoretical mathe-matics, Abell provides a rigorous way of connecting actors to actions, of linking such "compact" narrative units together in weak temporally ordered larger narratives (endowed with both local and global meaning), and of depicting them through directed graphs and matrices (Abell, 1987, pp. 52–61; 1993). You will not find in Abell's work any reference to the large body of linguistic literature on narrative or an acknowledgment of issues of meaning or how to map surface sentence structures onto his gram-mar. His work is grounded in logic and in a sociological theory of action. Nonetheless, Abell's work is full of precious insights. In his matrix and graph representation, you find the ingredients of network models, which were making their bold entrance in sociology around that time as an alternative methodological approach to the General Linear Model. Abell (1987) touches on issues of sequences—sequential and consequential actions—and of the fundamental relational properties of narrative (pp. 83–84); he discusses problems of aggregation of acts expressed by different verbs or verb phrases (e.g., kill, slain, murder, wound) into broader and more abstract categories (e.g., violence) (pp. 62–86). Abell (1987, pp. 87–91; 2004) further argues for the role of narrative—or at least a formalized narrative—as a way of overcoming shortcomings of the variable-centered approach. It is unfortunate that the combination of a mathematical approach, symbols typically unfamiliar to sociologists, and the lack of substantive applications,[29] not to mention the lack of a software package that would allow scholars to implement the approach, may have prevented Abell's work from gaining a wider audience.

Carley's (1993) work offers a way out of the limitations of the traditional content analysis approach to texts based on thematic categories and their relative frequencies by focusing on both themes and relations. Carley's Network Textual Analysis (NTA) "is based on the assumption that language and knowledge can be modeled as networks of words and their relations between them" (Diesner & Carley, 2004, p. 1). In the case of general texts, these relations further provide conceptual maps of the concepts that go hand in hand; in the case of narrative texts, these relations provide a map of the social relations among social actors.[30]

The sequential organization of narrative structures, rather than the microstructure of narrative centered on actors and actions, has been central to Abbott's (1995) search for patterns of recurrent sequences. Propp (1928/1968) wrote long ago,

> The sequence of events has its own laws. Theft cannot take place before the door is forced. Insofar as the tale is concerned it has its own entirely particular and specific laws. The sequence of elements . . . is strictly *uniform*. Freedom within this sequence is restricted by very narrow limits which can be exactly formulated. (p. 22)

The method of analysis proposed by Abbott (Abbott & Barman, 1997; Abbott & Hrycak, 1990) allows investigators to bring out those uniform sequences (and not just in narrative). Bearman and Stovel (2000) similarly focus on narrative sequences and use a novel representation of narrative sequences as networks to shed light on the process of identity formation for the Nazis. Their in-depth analysis of one short Nazi autobiographical account, based on the networks between elements (or clauses) in the text, highlights the fundamental structural differences between the two parts of the story: the *becoming* a Nazi and *being* a Nazi. Only in the becoming do specific cognitive elements[31] play the role of binding together the elements of the story, providing a unified and densely connected network. It is the lack of such cognitive elements in the *being* story that leads to atomized and broken network structures. Most important, the network representation of narrative sequences reveals narrative strategies perhaps "invisible" to the narrator himself. Smith (2007) uses that same network approach to great effect to tease out the different structures of Italians' and Slavs' conflicting narratives of their past, in the border region of Istria.[32]

Protest Event Analysis (PEA)

In the past few decades, protest event analysis (PEA) has been developed to systematically map, analyze, and interpret the occurrences and properties of large numbers of protests by means of content analysis, using sources such as newspaper reports and police records. (Koopmans & Rucht, 2002, p. 231; see also Koopmans & Statham, 1999)

For Koopmans and Rucht (2002), PEA "is a method that allows for the quantification of many properties of protest, such as frequency, timing and duration, location, claims, size, forms, carriers, and targets, as well as immediate consequences and reactions" (p. 231).

A key characteristic of the approach is its reliance on coding schemes based on actors and their actions, more specifically, on a seven-element structure made up of location (where and when), claimant (who), the addressee (to whom), the issue (what), the target (for/against whom), and the justification (why), expressed "in grammatical terms . . . as a *subject-action-addressee-action-object-justification clause* sequence" (Koopmans, Statham, Giugni, & Passy, 2005, pp. 254–255). Wada (2004), in his study of Mexican protest movements between 1964 and 2000, similarly "employs protest-event analysis of newspaper data" (pp. 245–246), on the basis of a "Subject-Verb-Object (SVO) 'Triplet' scheme to extract the information from the articles."

But whether one uses the label of *protest event analysis* or not, it is no doubt in the empirical study of social movements and protest events that a trickle of innovations in coding scheme design by Sorokin, Richardson, Eckstein, Gurr, Tilly, and Markoff led to coding schemes that displayed the structural characteristics of a story grammar.[33] And that is true *even when little or no reference is made to the body of linguistic work on narrative.*

One Good Reason

Question

Why do so many content analysis coding schemes, from different scholarly traditions, from early schemes in psychology to the more recent schemes in the study of protest events, end up looking alike, centered on actors and their actions, much like a story grammar?[34]

Answer

There is one good reason why many coding schemes seem to all look alike, along the lines of a story grammar. These schemes reflect a similar underlying linguistic structure of the texts they try to capture—texts that fundamentally belong to the narrative genre. And since narrative is characterized by an invariant linguistic structure centered on actors and their actions in time and space, not surprisingly, coding schemes that attempt to capture those texts end up adopting a similar SAO structure. Most scholars who have adopted coding schemes that look like story grammars have done so with little or no knowledge of the literature on narrative. Rather, the similarity in the texts they study—narrative—and the invariant structure of these texts—namely, actors doing some actions—forces itself on these scholars in the form of coding schemes that are nothing but story grammars.

Question and Answer (Which Structure?)

Question

Which "invariant" structure are we really talking about? We have seen several of these invariant structures, not one; from such macrostructures as Propp's 31 functions (reduced to 5 by Greimas and to 3 by Colby) to Labov's six functional parts of narrative (orientation, complication, evaluation, resolution, and coda) or the simple micro SAO structure. All these different "structures" have all been sold as "invariant," and yet they are all different from each other.

Answer

True. There are several different structures not just in narrative but, more generally, in any kind of text, both macro- and microstructures. As van Dijk has argued, all texts are characterized by macrostructures ("schema") that provide the "global schematic form" of a discourse. A text is not just a sequence of unrelated sentences, however syntactically well formed. A text is a unitary whole, with sentences organized around a dominant theme and topics within this whole. Different schemata characterize different text genres (van Dijk, 1983, p. 24). Thus, the schema of a research article is made up of the following macrostructural functional categories: introduction, statement of the problem and literature review, data and method, empirical results, discussion, and conclusions (see Gross, Harmon, & Reidy, 2002, p. 184). A research proposal contains functional parts such as aims and objectives, statement of the problem and literature review, research questions and hypotheses, research design (with methods of data collection and data analysis), project significance, expected outcomes, feasibility, and timetable. News articles are also characterized by fairly fixed, deep macrostructures, made up of a summary and a story; the story further comprises a situation and comments; the situation comprises episode and background; the episode includes both main events and consequences; and the background includes context (circumstances and previous events) and history (van Dijk, 1988, pp. 51–59; see also van Dijk, 1983, 1985).

At the microlevel, the SAO structure is a *semantic* structure despite some terminological confusion (S and O—Subject and Object—are syntactic categories, and A is a semantic category, an action, rather than a syntactic verb).[35] Although that basic structure is invariant, both its complexity and the labels of the various objects that make up the structure (namely, the SAO modifiers) may vary. In a labor conflict narrative, you are unlikely to find the color of people's eyes or hair, or their height. But these personal characteristics are typical of fairy tales and children stories (together with their witches, elves, gremlins, magical rings, and talking horses).

Syntactical microlevel linguistic structures may have also been relevant in the process of quantitative measurement of meaning. Consider the starting point of Chomsky's transformational syntax, the sentence S, rewritten in terms of noun phrases (NP) and verb phrases (VP).

$$S \rightarrow NP\ VP$$

The complexity of this simple structure can vary considerably, from the simplest sentence based on one clause only and elementary NP and VP to much more complex structures characterized by a number of embedded clauses within a sentence. The English language of scientific writing over the last centuries has shown a tendency toward greater sentence simplicity: Both sentence length (in terms of number of words) and sentence structure (in terms of clause density) have reduced. Furthermore, there has been a marked tendency toward very complex noun phrases, characterized by a number of string-linked nouns and adjectives.[36]

Even within narrative texts, you can search for many different things and for many different purposes. You could focus on the narration itself or on the narrator(s) (who narrates) and the narratee(s) (the narrative audience or whom it is narrated to). It makes a difference if a child narrates a story (with its altogether characteristic naïve sequence of "and then . . . ," "and then . . . ," "and then . . ."; story and plot coincide in these elementary narratives), a master storyteller such as a novelist (with maximum plot development), or an academic scientific writer (where analytic passages tend to dominate over rare narrative ones; and yet even analytical prose, even a scientific journal article, ultimately tells a story in a grand narrative format[37]). Similarly, it makes a difference if the narrative is aimed at children, adults, a learned audience, or specialized scientists. Or even why the story is told. Narrators and narratees constrain *how* events are narrated. The focus on *how* involves a focus on plot (rather than story), on rhetorical efficacy, on the strategic mix of pure narrative, description, and evaluation, and on the effective use of language (which adjectives, which verbs, which sentence construction—active or passive—are used).

All these are extremely important characteristics of a narrative text, closely linked to forms of representations, people's *mentalité,* their way of thinking. But the research question I am interested in is what people do, rather than what they think or feel. Focusing on what people do implies focusing on narrative proper, on the sequence of actions (see Figure 2.1). This zooming in on narrative proper has the advantage that its surface linguistic structure has invariant properties—namely, the 5 Ws—that can be exploited effectively to bring linguistic rigor in the use of narrative in sociohistorical research.

Question and Answer (What If My Texts Are Not Narrative?)

Question

It is quite clear that QNA works well with narrative texts only, and with narrative proper at that. Yet narrative may also contain description and evaluation. Furthermore, my documents, while containing some narrative, are mostly analytical. Is there anything I can do to overcome the limits of QNA?

Answer

You are right. QNA works well with narrative texts only (namely, any text that tells a story; see Figure 2.1). Although narrative comprises a large body of texts of interest to social scientists, these texts do not exhaust the range of documents that have been used in content analysis (e.g., newspaper editorials, corporate documents, university mission statements, religious or political speeches, party manifestos). A story grammar is ill-suited to the more analytical prose of these types of texts, based as they are on abstract concepts, rather than on actors and their actions, and on a sentence structure more complex than the simple canonical form of the language typical of narrative. And even narrative texts are rarely made up of purely narrative sentences (of someone doing something pro or against someone else). Evaluative and descriptive clauses will mix freely with narrative clauses. Again, a story grammar is ill-suited to capturing the language of evaluation and description. What's to be done?

More Linguistics

Linguistics would no doubt be my first port of call. Linguistics, after all, provided the theoretical foundations of our story grammar. It has hardly exhausted its bag of tricks. Consider Halliday's classification of processes (verbs), which was discussed earlier. Halliday (1985/1994) lists not just material and behavioural processes (the ones that make up skeleton narrative clauses, since they convert into verbs of doing), but also relational processes (pp. 119–130). Relational processes, of "being" and "having," provide definitions and characterizations. As such, these processes could be used to study how social actors construct their identity, how they identify and characterize themselves vis-à-vis others. They could be used, in other words, to study discourse rather than action, doing rather than saying. And that's exactly what Vicari (2008) did in her work on the master frames of transnational network coalitions (Social Fora).

Relying on Halliday's classification of processes, Vicari constructs a simple grammar of six actors (the forum itself; its participants, allies and enemies; its super actor, or the inspirational advocacy entity; and the "collective we," or the sense of community) and six types of actions (two based on relational processes of being and having, and four based on material processes). To get at the discourse of even action clauses (the purely narrative ones), to the saying behind the doing, Vicari uses the auxiliary and modal verbs that may accompany verbs of doing to construct a typology of narrative passages as "actual" (no modal verb present), "duty" (modal must or have to), "potential" (can or could), and "intentional" (will or want to).[38]

Vicari's use of Halliday's work on types of processes can be expressed in the following set of rewrite rules:

<Hallidays' process type>	→	<material> | <relational>
<material>	→	<verbal predicate>
<verbal predicate>	→	<action> | <intentional> | <modal>
<action>	→	<verb>
<verb>	→	went | mobilize | . . .
<intentional>	→	<auxiliary> <infinitive>
<auxiliary>	→	will | want to | . . .
<infinitive>	→	achieve | go | . . .
<modal>	→	<duty> | <potential>
<duty>	→	<auxiliary> <infinitive>
<auxiliary>	→	must | have to | . . .
<potential>	→	<auxiliary> <infinitive>
<auxiliary>	→	can | could | . . .
<relational>	→	<verbal predicate> | <nominal predicate>

\<verbal predicate\>	→	\<characterization\>
\<characterization\>	→	\<have tense\> \<direct object\>
\<have tense\>	→	has | had | have | . . .
\<direct object\>	→	power | strength | . . .
\<nominal predicate\>	→	\<definition\>
\<definition\>	→	\<copula\> \<nominal part\>
\<copula\>	→	is | was | were | . . .
\<nominal part\>	→	global | local | . . .

Using PC-ACE, Vicari coded 5,462 clauses taken from a sample of 222 Social Fora declarations of intent extracted from the web sites of World Social Forum chapters. Vicari's empirical results, based on exploratory statistical work, GIS, and network models for relational processes of characterization and definition, show the influence of local environments in the way fora define themselves and their targets, despite a shared collective frame. They also show that descriptive passages contain mostly definition processes (being) rather than characterization processes (having). Following Halliday, this suggests that social fora employ identifying rather than attributive constructions and that their descriptive contents provide actors with identities rather than just qualities. Organizations (in particular, traditional organizations, such as trade unions or political parties), rather than self-generated groups or other civic actors, are the most common allies. The enemies' list is long and varied, from abstract enemies (e.g., globalization or neoliberalism) to transnational institutions (e.g., G8, World Bank), multinational corporations, and individuals (e.g., G. W. Bush). But besides these common enemies, each forum also tackles its own reality of contextual, local-level enemies.

Vicari's network models of intention, duty, and potential relations highlight the idea that the injustice component is the real driving force of the World Social Forum collective action frame, the key for the self-identification of each network's node and the integration of agency and identity issues. In particular, from the network of duty relations, it seems that each social forum stresses the necessity of both local protest actions by its individual activists and transnational mobilization, rooted in more ephemeral cross-border collective protest. Framing resistance against enemies (the "injustice component") at the global level through universal demands helps framing resistance at the local level with particularistic demands.

Vicari's work has the merit of showing how story grammars can be profitably used to study discourse and not just action and how, once again, linguistics can provide tools for a rigorous study of discourse *even for purely narrative clauses.*

Turn to Rhetoric for Help

Rhetoric, like content analysis and quantitative narrative analysis, is also concerned with classifying parts of text, in a tradition that dates back to at least classical Greece, some 2,500 years ago. In contrast to content analysis, rhetoric is not concerned with "what" a text talks about (the "themes" of content analysis to be classified into the categories of a coding scheme). It is not even concerned with QNA's 5Ws—although the rhetorical tradition came up with the jingle *quis, quid, ubi, quibus auxiliis, cur, quomodo, quando*—which, in its English rendering, corresponds to the 5 Ws of journalism: who, what, when, where, why, and how (see Franzosi, 2004b, p. 217).

Rather, rhetoric is concerned with "how" a text talks about things, with how a text is written, not syntactically (the realm of grammar) but in terms of the forms of argumentation adopted, the ways in which a text attempts to persuade an audience. In its long life, rhetoric has accumulated an impressive classification of all "figures of speech." In Quintilian's words (first century AD), "Writers have given special names to all figures of speech" but, as in content analysis, "variously and as it pleased them."[39]

Rhetoric would be particularly useful in those applications of content analysis that analyze individuals' petitions to authorities in terms of their persuasive appeals—the proper domain of rhetoric—yet rhetoric there is nowhere to be found (e.g., Katz, Gurevitch, Danet, & Peled, 1969). Rhetoric is also nowhere to be found in a recent offshoot of content analysis and discourse analysis: frame analysis (for an overview, see Benford & Snow, 2000). Frames and frame analysis have come to mean many different things, some completely unrelated to text and discourse, some so broad as to end up overlapping/substituting older concepts with long scholarly traditions of their own, such as ideology or identity (Polletta & Kai Ho, 2006, pp. 6–9). While becoming a victim of its own success, with a proliferation of definitions, the concept of frame has kept one of its core meanings as the set of "persuasive devices" used by social actors in the tug and pull involved in the production of meaning (Polletta & Kai Ho, 2006, p. 9).

For Snow, Rochford, Worden, and Benford (1986, p. 464), "by rendering events or occurrences meaningful, frames function to organize experience and guide action." But despite Snow et al.'s reliance on key, classical rhetorical concepts such as "amplification," "appeal," and "justification," there is not a single reference to the tradition of rhetorical studies. Similarly, for Gamson and Modigliani (1989, p. 3), frames help "making sense of relevant events;" they provide the "central organizing idea" of interpretive packages that "have the task of constructing meaning over time" (Gamson & Modigliani, 1989, p. 4). And of course, social movement actors praise and blame other actors. But again, while these processes are studied and highlighted in the social movement literature, there is no attempt to understand them more broadly in terms of one of Aristotle's three branches of rhetoric: epideictic rhetoric, the rhetoric of praise and blame (see, however, Tilly, 2008). If the categories of rhetorical classification are the "figures of speech" and "the term *figure* . . . refers to any device or pattern of language in which meaning is enhanced or changed" (Lanham, 1991, p. 178), then rhetoric would clearly provide useful tools to frame analysts. After all, meaning is what these analysts are fundamentally concerned with.[40]

You can apply rewrite rules to specify the coding categories that will allow you to code basic information about the rhetorical forms of documents. For example,

<rhetoric >	→	<argumentation> <trope> <epideictic>
<argumentation>	→	<type of argument> <basis of argument>
<type of argument>	→	*ad personam* | ad hominem | . . .
<basis of argument>	→	science | religion | ethics | efficiency | . . .
<trope>	→	metaphor | metonymy | synecdoche | irony
<epideictic>	→	<blame> <praise>
<blame>	→	<who/what> <reason>
<who/what>	→	<actor> <concept>

Blame is what the *Avanti!* article of the fascist attack in Lucca uses. It does so by relying on one of the four master tropes (metaphor, metonymy, irony, and synecdoche): irony. Konstancya Walerych blames her sister or, more generally, American society (her justification) for not sending money home to her parents.

Rhetoric, particularly epideictic rhetoric, may be well suited to capturing those elements of narrative not easily captured by a story grammar (e.g., evaluation). In a rhetorical view of evaluation, the rewrite rules of this narrative element provided earlier as

<evaluation>	→	negative | positive | neutral

may be too simplistic.

Evaluation may be constructed as the result of a complex disposition of words in a conceptual space. The article that appeared in the *Atlanta*

Daily World on April 29, 1936, on Mr. Shaw's lynching as described earlier provides a good case in point. Many concepts go together in that article and with different sentiments attached to each, in a constellation of concepts that, together, ultimately provide a strong negative evaluation of lynching (from the courts to the inaction of states, the state of Georgia in particular; the need for the federal government's intervention; law and order; everyone's entitlement to a speedy and fair trial; newspapers' opposition to people's taking the law into their own hands at their will; lynching as evil, as a menace to the foundation of our government, as a blot on civilization, as an insult to constituted authority, as unsafe for democracy).[41]

In a conceptual space, a concept will be related to other concepts by specific types of relation, and it may be evaluated in specific ways, by itself or as part of the entire conceptual space. This view of a conceptual space can be expressed by the following set of rewrite rules:

<evaluation>	→	<conceptual space >
<conceptual space>	→	{{{<concept>} [<relation>]} [<sentiment>]}
<relation>	→	list/sequential | causal/consequential | . . .
<sentiment>	→	negative | positive | neutral

And Don't Forget Content Analysis

Linguistics. Rhetoric. But content analysis can also help—that content analysis that we had abandoned at the beginning of the book in search of a more rigorous approach to text coding grounded on the invariant linguistic properties of text, rather than on the varying interests of individual investigators. Yet for those linguistic elements that do not fit easily into the categories of a story grammar, the ad hoc nature of content analysis approach to text can still come handy . . . with one recommendation.

Relations! Relations! Relations!

Go back to content analysis, if you must, but try to adopt QNA's use of rewrite rules for the specification of stringent relations between coding categories. In content analysis, the categories of a coding scheme, mainly designed to capture what a text talks about (the "themes"), are typically listed seriatim, one after the other, with little or no relation to each other (at most, they are embedded, one into the other, in groups and subgroups). But texts are fundamentally relational. Ricoeur (1984, pp. 54–55), Burke (1945/1969, p. xv), Carley (1993), and Smith (2007) all insist on the fundamental relational nature of concepts in a text (see also Popping's (2000, pp. 97–127) chapter on "Network Text Analysis").

Narrative texts are doubly relational. They depict both *social relations* and *conceptual relations*. Social actors are related to other social actors via their actions (in a network of an actor's social relations, from Konstancya Walerych's parents, sister, and employment relations to Lint Shaw's Jim Crow Southern world of the mob, the white Georgians, and the assaulted white woman). Besides social relations, concepts and ideas also stand in relation to each other, with words distributed in conceptual spaces. It is one thing to be able to say which (and perhaps how often) themes, concepts, actors appear in a text and another to be able to map the network of relations that give meaning to a text (or the social world).

Whether you are interested in social relations (narrative of action) or in conceptual relations (narrative of discourse), build these relations in your grammar with the help of rewrite rules.

And Rewrite Rules

QNA starts with a story grammar.[42] In designing your own grammar, start with the basic SAO structure (the semantic triplet), and then ask yourself the question, How many hierarchical levels do I want (to put it differently, how many levels of aggregation do I want)? One? Two? Event and dispute (or campaign, with a set of events under it)? Once you have made that decision, start from your highest-level object (let's say, the <dispute>) and rewrite it, down to the Subject, Action, and Object. At this point, you need to ask yourself another question: How much detail do I want to have for my story grammar? In other words, how many modifiers for the S, A, and O do I want, beyond the obvious ones (such as time and space, reason, instrument, and outcome of action)?

Once you have developed a story grammar for the purely narrative passages of your documents, you need to ask yourself another question: Besides narrative proper, do I also want to code information on description and evaluation (e.g., relating concepts in a conceptual space) or on rhetoric? Whatever you decide, apply rewrite rules for *all* the objects in your grammar, all the categories in your coding scheme. As you keep rewriting the objects of your grammar, left to right, rewrite rules will help you keep your structure tight, avoiding unnecessary repetitions of objects in your structure, and establishing stringent relationships between objects. *Relations (and hierarchies) and rewrite rules go hand in hand in quantitative narrative analysis.*

Story Sequences (The Main Points About Narrative)

It is time for a pause. Time to ask ourselves, What have we learned? The story of what we have learned goes something like this, in the sequence of my story:

1. Narrative is one of many different available text genres; it is found across a range of products of human activity (paintings, sculptures, films, texts) and, more specifically, across different types of texts (poetry, letters, biographies, novels, . . .).

2. Narrative is fundamentally a story; it deals with events as happenings.

3. These happenings and events concern mostly human beings (although anthropomorphic beings, such as gremlins and elves, are popular in folktales and children's stories); narrative, in other words, typically concerns human experience and deals with human events; although events centered on nonhuman characters are possible (lightning, volcanoes, tsunamis, and earthquakes are often imputed with agency; e.g., "the earthquake in the Chinese province of Sichuan killed more than 69,000 people and injured nearly 400,000 people"), they are not most typical of narrative; events are typically expressed in terms of human actions (someone doing something).

4. There is little difference between events and actions, although, typically, events denote actions with a longer temporal duration (also referred to as macroactions as opposed to microactions; the microactions "walk out," "leaflet," and "picket" make up the larger macroaction, or event, "strike"); indeed, events and actions are denoted linguistically by verbs (as opposed to nouns, for instance).

5. Given the centrality of action (without action there is no narrative), both description and evaluation play a subordinate role in narrative; however, much textual space may be taken up by these subordinate narrative categories.

6. In narrative, actions (or events) are organized sequentially (either chronological sequences, as in story, or rhetorical sequences, as in plot); given the central role of temporal sequences in narrative, time is one of the fundamental categories of narrative, as denoted by the characteristic opening of stories ("once upon a time").

54

7. Space occupies a role subordinate to time in narrative theory (while time is a condition sine qua non of narrative—no time, no narrative—there can be narrative without space, at least not an explicit space); yet *social actors move in both space and time; if you are using QNA for historical research, both time and space should be fundamental categories of your story grammar.*

8. More generally, action, in narrative, is characterized by a set of circumstances that include time and space but also reason, outcome, instrument, and so on.

9. The sequential organization of events/actions (plot) leads, even if implicitly, to a story point: What is the point of the story? The evaluative function of narrative, when not explicitly present, is often implicitly contained in the story point; the story point (or the sequence of actions) may also provide a justification.

10. In narrative, the story must be coherent, both (or either) locally and globally; the story must make sense in its parts and as a whole.

11. In narrative, characters are subordinated to actions although there can be no action without an actor; the subordination of character to action in narrative, thus, implicitly involves the subordination of noun to verbs.

12. In the same way that action is qualified by its circumstances, characters are qualified by traits (e.g., physical, psychological, or professional characteristics).

13. The combination of actions and their circumstances, characters and their traits, constitutes the essential building block of narrative, the "skeleton narrative sentence"; this structure, often referred to as the 5 Ws (who, what, when, where, why, and how), is invariant across specific types of text (poem, letter, diary, etc.) and the infinite varieties of stories.

14. Narrative is characterized by *both* microlevel structures (the SAO, Subject-Action-Object, or 5 Ws structure) and macrolevel structures (story and plot but also Propp's, Greimas's, and Colby's functions or Labov's distinction of orientation, complication, evaluation, resolution, and coda or even the simple division of narrative proper, description, and evaluation).

15. Linguistics, rhetoric, and content analysis provide various tools that can be profitably used to overcome the limitations of QNA in its applicability to narrative text only.

This is what we have learned; or, at least, this is what I think we should have learned; after all, my plot—my way of telling you about narrative—may have confused this sequence of learning points (the story).

Notes

1. I am grateful to Tim Liao for bringing to my attention the narratives contained in this classic, *The Polish Peasant.*
2. Labov (1972, pp. 359–361; see also Labov & Waletzky, 1967, p. 20); Rimmon-Kenan (1983, pp. 2–3); Cohan and Shires (1988, pp. 52–53); Toolan (1988, p. 7).
3. Tomashevski (1925/1965, p. 70); Labov (1972); Prince (1973, p. 23); Bal (1977, p. 7); Todorov (1971/1977, p. 111); Rimmon-Kenan (1983, p. 19); Cohan and Shires (1988, p. 53–54).
4. At the level of plot the events of a story can form complex sequences by combining events in a variety of ways through enchainment, embedding, and joining (see Bremond, 1966; Todorov, 1968/1981, pp. 52–53; Rimmon-Kenan, 1983, p. 23).
5. See Benveniste (1966/1971, pp. 206–208); Barthes (1966/1977); a terminology then exported to the English world as *story* versus *discourse*, see Chatman (1978, p. 19); on story/plot, story/discourse, see Toolan (1988, pp. 11–12).
6. Most change would involve no such reversal of polarity, just an "after" different from the "before" but neither necessarily better nor worse.
7. On the reversal of situation, see Tomashevski (1925/1965, pp. 70–71); Todorov (1971/1977, pp. 111–112; 1981, p. 51). Bremond (1966) also believed that all sequences are sequences of either improvement or deterioration (see the discussion by Rimmon-Kenan, 1983, p. 27).
8. Tomashevski (1925/1965, p. 70); Barthes (1966/1977, pp. 93–94); Chatman (1978, pp. 32, 53–56); Rimmon-Kenan (1983, p. 16).
9. Todorov (1968/1981, p. 41); Rimmon-Kenan (1983, pp. 17–19); Cohan and Shires (1988, pp. 17, 58).
10. The problem with Propp's or Greimas's schemata is that both reduce "narrative structure to functions denoting ONLY one macro-semantic category of the macro-proposition: ACTIONS" (van Dijk, 1972, p. 287). The arguments of the basic narrative function, such as subject and object, are not analyzed, presumably because the hero is the main protagonist of folktales. If we want to generalize the macrostructures to contexts where more than one actor plays a role, we need to introduce the different actants (subjects and objects) and their actions (van Dijk, 1972, p. 287). Furthermore, we need to show how deep structures (schemata) are related to higher-level structures.
11. "Eidons" are sequences of narrative thought. Colby's analysis is concerned with finding recurrent sequences of narrative elements, rather than simply identifying those elements (as in Propp's original work). Only a handful of the functions found by Propp in Russian folktales are also found in Eskimo folktales. Colby concludes, "the narrative elements and rules resulting from this analysis appear to apply to the folktales of all Eskimo, but not to the folktales of neighboring peoples. . . . [T]he set of Eskimo eidons is culture specific, not universal" (Colby, 1973, pp. 645–646).

56

12. For a comparison of Greimas's and Labov and Waletzky's schema, see van Dijk (1972, p. 293).

13. Cognitive psychologists also embraced the idea of narrative structures (e.g., Mandler, 1982; Rumelhart, 1975; for a review of this literature, see Franzosi, 2004b, pp. 45–47). In the psychologists' work on narrative and story grammars, there is nothing innovative from the linguistic viewpoint, but their experimental work on the validity of a story grammar approach to cognition shows that people use something like a story grammar when interpreting and recalling stories and that breakdown in comprehension occurs for stories not "conforming to an ideal schema . . . [not] matching a canonical structure" (Mandler, 1982, pp. 307–308).

14. Although, as Chatman (1978, pp. 47, 49) argues, readers will typically attempt to make a story out of even temporally sequenced but logically unrelated clauses by implicitly supplying logical connectives.

15. See the essays collected in Tully (1988).

16. Chatman also distinguishes events as *actions* and *happenings,* where actions are nonverbal physical acts, speeches, feelings, perceptions, and sensations (Chatman, 1978, pp. 44–45). Prince similarly distinguishes *stative* and *active* events, the former being events that describe a state, the latter an action (Prince, 1973, p. 29). Furthermore, a stative event, for Prince (1973), is expressed in a story by a stative sentence, that is, a sentence "which is not paraphrasable by a sentence of the form *NP's V-ing NP Aux be an act*" (p. 30). The sentence "John was happy" is stative because it cannot be paraphrased by "John's being happy was an act." Van Dijk (1972, p. 142) also distinguishes between two types of predicates, static and dynamic.

17. The linguists' distinction between doing and saying has generated a lively debate in the social movement literature between the proponents of action and of discourse as different research strategies in the study of social movements (Koopmans and Statham, 1999, pp. 203–204).

18. Todorov (1969, pp. 27–28; more generally, Todorov, 1969, pp. 27–41; 1971/1977, pp. 218–233; 1968/1981, pp. 48–51); Chatman (1978, p. 91); Prince (1973, pp. 32, 92–93).

19. Documents should be cross-referenced to every single object in the grammar and not just disputes although, for simplicity's sake, this has not been repeated for every object. It is the {<document>} that makes possible the identification of the source of any data item (e.g., for newspaper articles, newspaper name, date, page number, column, and position in the column). When working with a team of coders, the rewrite rules of every object should also contain the <coder name> and <coding date/time>.

20. The most comprehensive account of narrative time is Genette's (1972/1980) treatment. Ricoeur's (1984/1985/1988) three-volume treatment is more ambitious but not as crisp as Genette's. Ricoeur deals with linguists', philosophers', and historians' views of time. Ricoeur's work provides a comprehensive review of each author's position in a very lucid and clear language. For brief introductions to the issues, see Rimmon-Kenan (1983, pp. 43–58); Cohan and Shires (1988, pp. 84–89); and Toolan (1988, pp. 48–61).

21. The narrativists' duration and frequency do not just refer to the duration and frequency of the narrated (real-life) events. More generally, duration and frequency refer to the relationship between narrative clauses and narrated events. A narrator can sum up in one sentence events that took place over a long period of time ("After the fall of the Roman empire . . .") or dwell for many pages on fleeting events lasting a few minutes. A narrator can recount the same event several times (frequency). And that game is by no means confined to purely fictional narrative.

22. A clause is a grammatical unit that includes a predicate and an explicit or implied subject; a sentence is a grammatical unit that is composed of one or more clauses.

23. For more general advantages of a grammar-based approach, see van Dijk (1983, pp. 26–27).

24. See Krippendorf (1980, p. 84).

25. Markoff et al. (1975, p. 37); Shapiro and Markoff (1998, p. 64).

26. For example, "How many times a week would you say you drink alcoholic beverages?" Once a week; two or three times a week; every day; on weekends only?" as opposed to an open-ended question, such as "How many times a week would you say you drink alcoholic beverages?" which leaves respondents free to construct their answers.

27. Maynes, Pierce, & Laslett (2008). See also the chapters in standard methodological textbooks (Berg, 2004; Denzin & Lincoln, 1994, 2005; Taylor & Bogdan, 1984). For feminist methodology, with its strong emphasis on qualitative methods, see also Reinharz (1992).

28. In fact, the very way ethnographers write their scholarly accounts takes different narrative forms: the realist tale, the confessional tale, the impressionist tale (Van Maanen, 1988; on writing ethnography, see also the essays in Clifford & Marcus, 1986; Rosaldo, 1989/1993).

29. See Heise's (1993) critique on this point.

30. On a network approach to content analysis, see Popping (2000, pp. 97–127).

31. These are defined as those "aspects of the narrative in which the author questions the meanings of elements, draws conclusions, or reveals a new cognitive understanding about his situation" (Bearman & Stovel, 2000, p. 83).

32. Interesting work by Gibson (2005), although not necessarily dealing with narrative but with conversations and turn taking in conversation, is also similarly highly formalized and based on sequences and networks.

33. For the story of these innovations, see Franzosi (2004b, pp. 35–40).

34. For a discussion of some examples, see Franzosi (2008, pp. xxxii–xxxiii).

35. In fact, in my advice on coding, I recommended coding all relevant information as specified by the story grammar, regardless of its syntactic position in the text and regardless of any other type of information provided by the text but not specified in the grammar (e.g., evaluation or description).

36. On the changing language of scientific writing, see Gross et al. (2002).

37. Thus, a quantitative article on the content analysis of representations of women or African Americans in advertisements and commercials may be summarized

58

in such (grand) narrative sentences: "Women do not fare well in the world of advertisement, and they need to continue to fight for more equal treatment" and "Despite the inroads made by the civil rights movement, African Americans are far from having achieved equality." I am grateful to my student Linda Oyesiku for pointing this out to me.

38. Vicari's typology corresponds to Gamson's classification of protest framing dynamics into three components: injustice (duty), agency (potential), and identity (intentional). The injustice component expresses the moral indignation driving protest action. The agency component refers to the consciousness that societal conditions can be altered through collective action. The third component, concerned with identity issues, refers to the process of defining an intentional collective "we," in opposition to an external, adversarial "they" (Gamson, 1992, pp. 6–7).

39. *Omnibus scriptores sua nomina dederunt, sed varia et ut cuique fingenti placuit* (*Istitutio Oratoria,* Liber Nonus, LIV).

40. The study of rhetoric has enjoyed a revival in recent decades, after a long period of decline (but preceded by centuries of intense scholarly production). For a good list of rhetorical terms, see Lanham (1991). On classical rhetoric (Greek and Latin), see, for all, Kennedy (1994). For the modern period, see Roberts and Good (1993) and Vickers (1988). For analyses of rhetoric in the social sciences, see Edmondson (1984) and McCloskey (1985).

41. While the purely narrative elements of documents and their sequential organization in a story may cut across different documents (e.g., a particular protest described in several police reports and where perhaps only new information is coded from each document), rhetorical forms (and to some extent the conceptual space) are mostly features of specific documents: Specific documents build their arguments in specific rhetorical ways and build specific conceptual spaces (although a set of documents on a dispute/event will also contain overall rhetorical forms and overall conceptual spaces, and tracing their unfolding across documents may be a worthwhile exercise).

42. PC-ACE, the software used in this book to carry out QNA, comes with a simple built-in story grammar that you can export. You can find another example of story grammar in my book *From Words to Numbers* (Franzosi, 2004b, pp. 339–342). On my Web site, you can also find the more complex story grammar I used in my project on the rise of Italian fascism.

CHAPTER 3. COMPUTER STORAGE AND RETRIEVAL OF NARRATIVE INFORMATION

Question and Answer (Where Are the Numbers?)

Question

Where are the numbers in this quantitative narrative analysis? All we have seen is words: linguists' and literary critics' views on narrative, ways of structuring narrative into the categories of a story grammar. But how do you go from there to the numbers?

Answer

To get to the numbers, you need one more step, at least if you deal with large volumes of text: You need computer software that will allow you to store (and retrieve) the information of a narrative text into the categories of a story grammar. Indeed, without software, quantitative narrative analysis is not feasible, at least not on a large scale (consider the 18,000 documents of my project on Italian fascism analyzed in this book). The sheer complexity of the grammar in terms of the number of categories and their relational properties would confine the use of QNA to trivial examples. If "no software, no QNA," what are the options?

No Software, No QNA, No Numbers: Available Software Options

The number of software packages for the analysis of words is large and continually growing.[1] Those that make possible a computer implementation of a story grammar, however, are much fewer. Without any pretense to exhaustiveness, I review here some of the software options for quantitative narrative analysis. I review them in the order in which they would probably come to mind to you (indeed, put to me more or less in this order by interested users):

1. Fully automated approaches (KEDS and IDEA)

2. Popular, commercially available software for computer-assisted qualitative data analysis (CAQDAS, e.g., ATLAS.ti, N6, NVivo, MAXQDA, WinMax); although I focus on ATLAS.ti for illustrative purposes, these CAQDAS programs all work in very similar ways (for a comparison, see Lewins & Silver, 2007; for a comparison in terms of QNA, see Franzosi et al., 2009)

3. Software that shares QNA's language of actors and actions (ETHNO or AutoMap)

4. QNA in a simple spreadsheet

5. QNA in a relational database

6. A ready-made relational database, PC-ACE (Program for Computer-Assisted Coding of Events)

Each option has advantages and disadvantages, although in different proportions. PC-ACE probably offers the most comprehensive approach to quantitative narrative analysis, but CAQDAS packages as well do allow a minimal implementation of QNA.

The Tasks Involved in QNA (How Software Can Help)

Quantitative narrative analysis, not differently from traditional quantitative content analysis or even computer-assisted *qualitative* data analysis of texts (field notes or transcripts of interview data, oral and life histories, and focus groups), involves several different tasks: data coding, data verification and cleaning, data aggregation, data query, and data analysis. What do these tasks entail?

Data Coding

Coding refers to the task of assigning specific parts of a text (e.g., a single word such as *kill* or a set of words such as *tie down*, a clause, a sentence, a paragraph, or an entire document) to one of the coding categories of your coding scheme (in CAQDAS programs, a coding category is typically referred to as "code" and the coding scheme as "code system," a language that you also find in Glaser and Strauss's (1967) seminal vade mecum for qualitative researchers).

Notice: data coding is preceded by several different tasks that are not, however, part of computer-assisted software of textual analysis. In particular, the texts to be content-analyzed have to be selected and made available to coders for coding. If the content analysis software expects to import documents into the software (in MS Word or ASCII format), these documents must be available in digitized form. Recorded interview transcripts must be transcribed; paper, microfilm, or image documents must be digitized. This can be a lengthy and time-consuming process. Microfilms can be printed or converted to image form, but depending on the readability of the original, converting a microfilm page to a Word document may be very time consuming. If your documents are in printed form, you can scan each page into a pdf file and convert this into a Word document or a text (ASCII) file.[2] OCR (optical character recognition) technology of this kind is not perfect; so, expect some hand editing after scanning your documents in. Line-by-line OCR technology (like the handheld C-pen line scanner) may also be a viable solution for you. Unless you have a huge amount of text to turn into digital form, this technology does wonders. And, of course, by the time you read this book, new technological solutions to the problem of digitizing text may have become available (e.g., voice recognition software with 100% reliability).

Data Verification and Cleaning

Data coding, like any human activity, is subject to error (e.g., a segment of text assigned to the wrong code or not assigned to a code when it should have been). You need to inspect your coded data for errors (verification), and if you catch any errors, you need to "clean" them (i.e., remove the errors). Data verification and cleaning should be simultaneous with data coding, but expect further data cleaning after the completion of coding.

Data Aggregation

In QNA, data coding is highly disaggregated. The coding categories/ codes used are "functional" categories of narrative discourse (e.g., actors, actions, time, space), rather than theoretical categories that reflect the researcher's specific needs and questions. When dealing with large volumes of textual data, this may lead to thousands of distinct words/textual expressions for any of these categories. For the purpose of data analysis, of finding meaningful patterns in your data, you need to reduce further the dimensions of your data (indeed, a process often referred to as "data reduction" in the social sciences and as "linguistic categorization" in linguistics), by aggregating individual textual elements into broader categories.

Data Query

With your data in a computer environment, in some form of database, you need to be able to access those data (e.g., for data verification and data analysis). You need to be able to extract specific items of stored data—a process known as data query in database jargon. You should be able to query your data in ways as general as possible. In a computer environment, there are different ways of storing information (e.g., your documents, segments of texts, codes) and with different properties (e.g., storage efficiency, speed of access of information, type of information you can access). The way your computer software organizes data will affect the way you can query your data.

Data Analysis

Strictly speaking, you should not expect a content analysis software package to have complex data analysis features. There are too many and too many different types of analyses—statistical and nonstatistical—to be included in a content analysis software package. You certainly would not want a content analysis software package to include sophisticated statistical routines. There are plenty of excellent data analysis packages out there (from general statistical packages such SPSS, STATA, and R to more specialized software packages, such as UCINET or Pajek for network analysis or ARCGIS or the popular freeware GRASS for spatial analyses). What you do want is for your content analysis software to allow you to export your data in ways easily handled by specialized data analysis software. Again, data storage and data query and export are tightly interrelated.

It is in the completion of these tasks that computer software can greatly help (particularly for large volumes of texts).

The Ideal Option: Do It Automatically (KEDS and IDEA)

One of the drawbacks of content analysis, where coding is carried out by human coders, is its high labor costs (at least for large projects). Because of this, content analysis has spearheaded the development of automated applications of text processing. Some of these applications have been developed for the purpose of picking up themes in a text in a classical approach to content analysis (e.g., Stone's *General Inquirer,* developed in the early 1960s, or Laver and collaborators' more recent *Wordscores,* "a novel approach to extracting dimensional information from political texts using computerized content analysis").[3] Other applications, however, have attempted to parse sentences automatically in a simple SVO structure, in an approach that comes very close to the approach to narrative illustrated in this book. Two projects—KEDS (Kansas Event Data System; Schrodt, 2006) and IDEA (Integrated Data for Events Analysis; Bond, Jenkins, Taylor, & Schock, 1997; Bond, Bond, Oh, Jenkins, & Taylor, 2003)—get at "*who* does *what,* to/for *whom,*" by recording the subject, verb, and object of the lead sentences of wire news reports on international events such as diplomatic exchanges and military attacks.

Beware! Don't Multiply Historical Events

Despite the relative success of KEDS or IDEA, computer automation of narrative texts is not quite there yet.[4] Automatic parsing delivers only the constitutive elements of a story grammar. It tends to break down when dealing with complex sentence structures. It leads to a potential duplication of events. Indeed, it is one thing to study discourse and representations (whether of media or other sources); and it is another thing to treat those representations as a marker of historical reality. As discourse, the repeated reference to an event (let's say a fascists' assault on the Socialist Party headquarters) in an article printed in the socialist newspaper *Avanti!* is a sign of the emphasis placed by the journalist on the event, perhaps a sign of moral outrage. Thus, a frequency of 8 for the event "assault" (or a frequency of 8 of the semantic triplet "fascists assault socialist newspaper *Avanti!*"), as picked up by an automatic text processing routine, can be correctly interpreted as a marker of the journalist's use of the rhetorical figure of amplification. But the event occurred only once in history. You cannot count it as eight different events if you use this number to gauge the intensity of certain types of events in time and space. At the current state of the art of text processing of automatic software packages such as KEDS or IDEA, the SVO structure is parsed as many times as it appears in the original text. As a result, every duplicate SVO structure will need to be carefully inspected (and eliminated) if the parsed data are taken as a signifier of what happened in history.

Computer-Assisted Qualitative Data Analysis Software (CAQDAS)

If an automatic solution to QNA is out of the question (at least, for now), popular, commercially available qualitative data analysis software packages could perhaps at least help in making the process easier (although not labor free). Over the past two decades, this type of software has grown in number, power, and ease of use. Brand names such as ATLAS.ti, N6 (ex NUD*IST, no doubt a sexier logo), NVivo, MAXQDA, and WinMax have become standard icons among qualitative data analysts dealing with large volumes of field notes, or answers to in-depth interviews or focus groups (for a comparative analysis of this type of software, see Lewins & Silver, 2007; for a comparison of PC-ACE and CAQDAS programs in relation to QNA, see Franzosi et al., 2009). This new generation of Windows computer packages for general textual analysis is very useful for setting up coding categories ("codes"), for identifying and coding the themes present in a text (or set of texts), and then providing frequency distributions of coding categories.[5]

Figure 3.1 shows an ATLAS.ti screen shot with a list of available codes on the right and the text to be coded on the left (in our case, the Lucca fascists' story taken from *Avanti!*). Coding is done by selecting a portion of the text and then assigning it to a code (e.g., the selected text to the code Triplet).

Within the selected (and coded) triplet, you then highlight the actor "fascists" and assign it to the code Participant:Actor:Fascists. You proceed that way for every object to be coded within the triplet and for every triplet in the document, and the fully coded newspaper article will look like this (Figure 3.2).

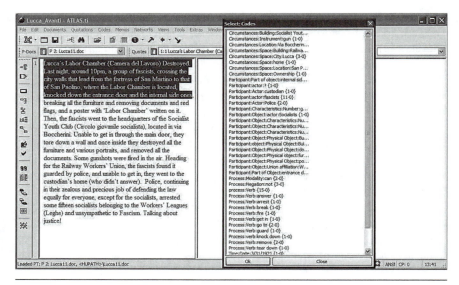

Figure 3.1 Coding in ATLAS.ti

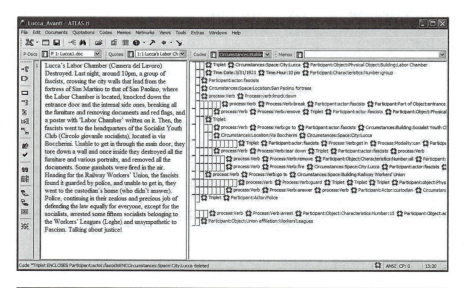

Figure 3.2 The Fully Coded Article in ATLAS.ti

Querying the Codes

Coding is no doubt easy in ATLAS.ti and similar software. But, of course, one codes to query the codes, interrogate them, in search of patterns. The query tools of ATLAS.ti, indeed, allow you to do just that: Ask questions such as "What did the fascists do in Lucca?" You start by querying for all the triplets enclosing the code Participant:Actor:Fascists (see Figure 3.3).

The result of the query generates a "supercode" that can then be further queried, basically asking the query tool to display all the triplets enclosing the supercode Participant:Actor:Fascists and enclosing the code Circumstances:Space:City:Lucca (see Figure 3.4).

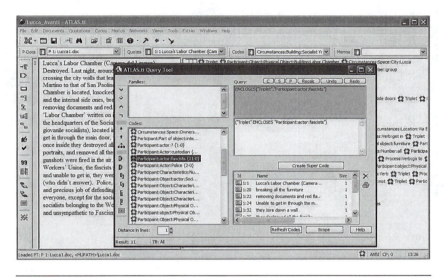

Figure 3.3   Data Query in ATLAS.ti (Participant:Actor:Fascists{11-0})

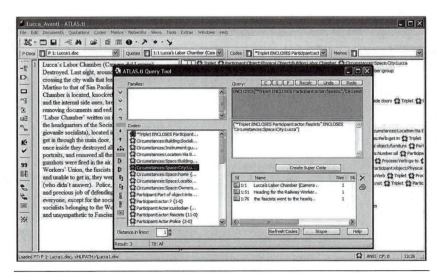

Figure 3.4   Data Query in ATLAS.ti (Circumstances:Space:City:Lucca)

66

Finally, the supercode generated by the query, will be queried again to show all the Process:Verb "within" it (Figure 3.5).

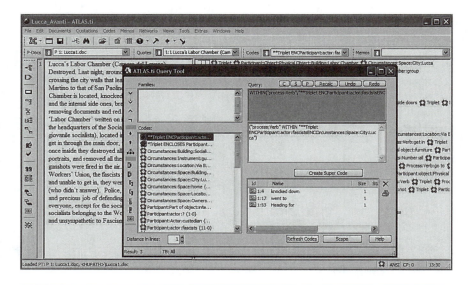

Figure 3.5   Data Query in ATLAS.ti (**TripletENCParticipant:acto)

The query report, containing a list of quotes extracted by the query (Figure 3.6), shows that ATLAS.ti allows you to retrieve information about the basic elements of a narrative (e.g., who and what).

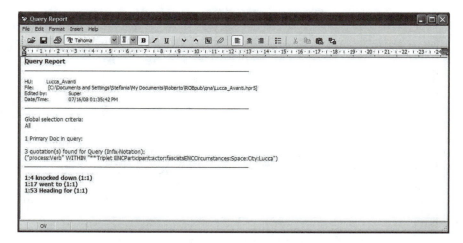

Figure 3.6   Quotes Extracted by the Query Tool in ATLAS.ti

Further Options? ETHNO and AutoMap

Besides ATLAS.ti, N6, Nvivo, MAXQDA, or WinMax, two noncommercial software packages—ETHNO and AutoMap[6]—have the appeal of being based on some of the familiar categories of a story grammar (e.g., ETHNO's Agents, Actions, Objects, and Instruments or AutoMap's agents, actions, and locations).[7] But the similarities are deceiving. The logic of these programs is different from QNA. ETHNO's aim is to force investigators to make explicit the implicit assumptions built into causal arguments, as reflected by the chronological sequence of skeleton narrative sentences.[8] It was not designed for the comparison of large numbers of narratives in large-scale projects. ETHNO focuses on a single text, forcing the investigator to make explicit the identification of sequential and consequential actions, to highlight the causal structure of arguments.

AutoMap was designed to extract meaning from texts by analyzing the frequencies and covariance of terms, concepts, and themes and the relations between them in the form of network maps. When the nodes of these network maps are concepts, AutoMap provides a snapshot of the mental map of a text's author. When the nodes are people, groups that people communicate with, organizations they join, or resources at their disposal, AutoMap reveals the structure of social and organizational systems. Proximity in the text of certain types of words is AutoMap's key organizing principle and its basis for analysis. You cannot organize the constitutive elements of the story grammar into chronologically ordered semantic triplets.

"Do-It-Yourself" Options

Question
If none of the available software options are optimally suited to quantitative narrative analysis, are there any "do-it-yourself" options?

Answer
There are two do-it-yourself options that scholars have used: spreadsheets and databases.

Spreadsheet Design

A rectangular organization of the data (as in spreadsheets) provides the simplest way to store information in a computer. Indeed, that has been the traditional computer data model used in statistical packages (with cases in rows and variables in columns). The linear structure of a rectangular data matrix should be adequate for storing the information of a very simple story grammar based on subject, action, object, and only a handful of attributes (e.g., time and space, reason, outcome). Oliver and Myers's work (1999) on newspaper coverage of protest events in Madison, Wisconsin, is a good case in point.[9]

More complex story grammars, based on a large number of objects, would run into problems with a rectangular data model. As Figure 3.7 shows, the implementation of QNA in a rectangular matrix may result in cells with empty values (when narrative categories are not present). More problematically, relationships between cell values across different rows cannot be easily established. A database implemented in a relational database management system (RDBMS, e.g., Oracle, FoxPro, and Microsoft ACCESS) represents a better alternative to rectangular design for storing and retrieving such complex data structures as a story grammar. What is a database?

	A	B	C	D	E	F	G	H	I	J	K	L	N
1	Event ID	Triplet ID	subject	number	organization	action	time	space	reason	object	object part	number	
2	1	1	fascists	group		knock down	3/21/1921	Lucca		Labor Chamber	door		
3	1	2	fascists	group		break	3/21/1921	Lucca		Labor Chamber	furniture	all	
4													
5													
6													

Figure 3.7   QNA in an Excel Spreadsheet

The RDBMS Alternative (and the Power of SQL)

A database is "nothing more than a system whose overall purpose is to record and maintain information," "a computer-based recordkeeping system," in the definition of C. J. Date (1981, p. 3), one of the early developers of database systems. The key characteristic of database design is that information is stored in separate tables, rather than in a single table as in spreadsheet design, with each table storing specific information (e.g., subjects in a subject_table, actions in an action_table). In RDBMS, information stored in separate tables is linked together via one overlapping field (or "column") between two different tables (Date, 1981, p. 65; these links between tables are technically called "relationships").

To see how an RDBMS works, let's design a very simple database that aims to store information on the basic SAO structure of a story grammar. We need a table for triplets (triplet_table), a table for subjects (subject_table), one for actions (action_table), and one for objects (object_table). We also need a table that stores the actual values found in the text (let's call this table dictionary_table). Figure 3.8 provides a graphical representation of the table structure of this simple database. It highlights the overlapping fields between any two tables, which is characteristic of relational database design (e.g., the triplet_ID in the subject_table, action_table, and object_table overlapping with the ID field of the triplet_table, or the dictionary_ID in the

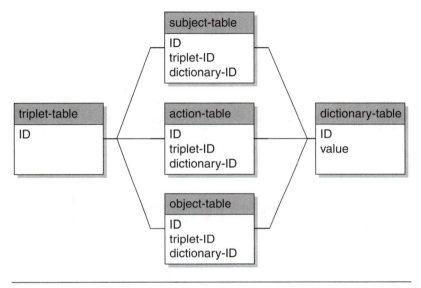

Figure 3.8   Basic Tables and Relationships in a Simple Database

subject_table, action_table, and object_table overlapping with the ID field of the dictionary_table).

Populated with values taken from the *Avanti!* article on the fascist attack in Lucca of March 31, 1921, these five tables (Tables 3.1, 3.2, 3.3, 3.4, and 3.5) would look like this.

Table 3.1   triplet_table of Sample RDBMS

ID
1
2
. . .
16

To extract information from this set of separate but interconnected tables, computer scientists have developed a simple and powerful language: SQL (Structured Query Language).[10] SQL is based on a handful of commands, in particular *select* (i.e., extract a specific field), *from* (a specific table), *where* (a condition set on specific values of selected fields for selected tables). Thus, the following SQL query extracts the ID of all occurrences of objects from the object_table for the fourth triplet,

70

select dictionary_ID

from object_table

where triplet_ID = 4,

yielding a list of three entries: 9, 10, 11.

Table 3.2 subject_table of Sample RDBMS

ID	triplet_ID	dictionary_ID
1	1	1
2	2	1
3	3	1
4	4	1
5	5	1
6	6	1
7	7	1
8	8	1
9	9	1
10	10	17
11	11	1
12	12	19
13	13	1
14	14	1
15	15	21
16	16	19

Table 3.3 action_table of Sample RDBMS

ID	triplet_ID	dictionary_ID
1	1	2
2	2	3
3	3	6
4	4	8

ID	triplet_ID	dictionary_ID
5	5	2
6	6	12
7	7	13
8	8	15
9	9	8
10	10	18
11	11	2
12	12	20
13	13	12
14	14	2
15	15	23
16	16	24

Table 3.4   object_table of Sample RDBMS

ID	triplet_ID	physical_object	dictionary_ID
1	2	True	4
2	2	True	5
3	3	True	7
4	4	True	9
5	4	True	10
6	4	True	11
7	7	True	14
8	8	True	7
9	8	True	16
10	9	True	9
11	12	True	21
12	16	False	25

72

Table 3.5 dictionary_table of Sample RDBMS

ID	Value
1	Fascists
2	Go
3	Knock down
4	Entrance door
5	Internal side doors
6	Break
7	Furniture
8	Remove
9	Documents
10	Red flags
11	Poster
12	Get in
13	Tear down
14	Wall
15	Destroy
16	Portraits
17	?
18	Fire
19	Police
20	Guard
21	Railway Workers' Union
22	Custodian
23	Answer
24	Arrest
25	Socialists

The function *count,* within a select clause, will allow us to compute the number of occurrences of a specific value, for example the number of times the dictionary entry with ID = 1 occurs in the subject_table, renamed as *frequency*:

select ID *as* frequency = *count*(ID)

from subject_table

where dictionary_ID = 1,

yielding a value of 12.

The real power of SQL stems from its ability to link information across different tables (e.g., the subject_table and the dictionary_table via the overlapping field dictionary_ID in the subject_table and ID in the dictionary_table. The following SQL query extracts a list of all *distinct* subjects in our story:

select distinct dictionary_table.value

from subject_table, dictionary_table

where dictionary_table.ID = subject_table.dictionary_ID,

yielding four values: ?, custodian, fascists, police.

Finally, the following query provides a complete list of the subjects and their actions in our story:

select distinct	S_dictionary.value *as* SUBJECT,
	A_dictionary.value *as* ACTION
from	subject_table *as* S,
	dictionary_table *as* S_dictionary,
	action_table *as* A,
	dictionary_table *as* A_dictionary,
where	S.triplet_ID = A.triplet_ID *and*
	S.dictionary_ID = S_dictionary.ID *and*
	A.dictionary_ID = A_dictionary.ID

SUBJECT	ACTION
fascists	go
fascists	knock down
fascists	break

fascists	remove
fascists	cannot get in
fascists	tear down
fascists	destroy
?	fire
police	guard
custodian	answer
police	arrest

Thus, via SQL, we can query the database to extract information in very general ways. But which queries should we pose of a database designed for quantitative narrative analysis? Which questions do we want to ask?

Questions For/From a Story

Psychologists working on story comprehension and recall test their subjects' understanding of a story they have read by asking them questions about that story.[11] Who were the characters of the story? What did these various characters do? What role did they play in the story (primary/secondary)? What were the relations between characters? For what reason did they behave the way they did? Did any/some of the characters benefit (or suffer) from the actions of the other? Are there villains and heroes in the story? Which traits do these characters have (male, female, Italian, American, blue-eyed, good, evil)? When did the actions narrated in the story happen? Where? Were certain types of action committed by specific actors, at specific times or locations? Were there any actions in the story that, if taken out of the story, would change the course of events? These are the questions we want to ask via SQL. These are, indeed, the questions that anthropologists and qualitative social scientists ask of their data. A section of Dwyer's seminal work, *Moroccan Dialogues*, is titled "Some Questions about Events" (in the specific case, a theft event), and the questions are "Tell me what happened with that fellow who took the bicycle." "What do you think they will do with the thief?" "Was Tahami an 'Arobi'?" "Do they often steal?" "Sometimes you have Berbers who work for you; are they also deceitful?" "How many different kinds of Berbers are there?" (Dwyer, 1982, pp. 112–129).

A Word of Caution About the RDBMS Alternative

Of all the available options for implementing QNA, I should warn you against the do-it-yourself RDBMS option. Commercially available database software, such as Microsoft ACCESS, Oracle, or FoxPro, will allow you to build a simple database with minimal investment, even if you never thought of database systems before. You can design, relatively easily, the tables where the textual information is stored and the forms through which to enter that information. You can also build the SQL queries that will search the data once you have entered them—you can do this even without knowing any SQL; the MS ACCESS query wizard, for instance, allows you to build queries visually, and it will then convert them into SQL for you.

Yet it probably won't be long before you outgrow your simple design. You will want more flexibility in defining your story grammar (and changing it as your project proceeds). You will want greater data entry and data-retrieval speed (of the essence in large-scale data-collection projects). You will want greater data reliability (thus, programming for error trapping). If you employ a team of coders, you will want to keep track of what each user does in the database. It is at that point that the learning curve suddenly becomes very steep (that is true even for an experienced programmer). If you work with Microsoft ACCESS, you will need to learn VBA, the Visual Basic programming language, through which you can program what you need. It is the VBA code that gives you the real engine under the hood of what ACCESS allows you to see from the outside. Even what goes on over the hood will require you to make a major investment in learning ACCESS.

Don't fool yourself with the ease with which you can move the first steps in RDBMS design. And don't underestimate either the dangers of what historian Bailyn (1982, p. 6) called "mind-absorbing, soul-entrapping ... technical problem-solving" in his 1981 presidential address to the American Historical Association. Don't fall into the trap of displacing the means for the end. I speak from experience.

A Ready-Made RDBMS Option (PC-ACE)

PC-ACE (Program for Computer-Assisted Coding of Events, available for free download at www.pc-ace.com) is a software program that I designed to carry out quantitative narrative analysis for large-scale sociohistorical research (for a more in-depth, technical treatment, see Franzosi & Cunial, 2009). It is a Microsoft ACCESS application designed to deal with complex data structures in very flexible ways. Accordingly, you can use PC-ACE for a bibliography, a telephone directory, a company's parts or customer inventory, or a narrative.[12] I used PC-ACE myself to collect data from newspapers for several different substantive projects (differences between industrial- and service-sector labor conflicts in Italy, 1985–1986; lynchings in Jim Crow South, 1875–1930; rise of Italian fascism, 1919–1922). In this book, as a way of illustration, I focus on the project on the rise of Italian fascism.

*A PC-ACE Application to the Rise of
Italian Fascism (1919–1922)*

Of the years between 1919 and 1922, Tilly, Tilly, and Tilly (1975, p. 126) wrote that they "may well have produced the highest level of involvement in collective violence . . . in Italy's modern history." The uniqueness of those years in Italian history is clearly borne out by the time-series plot of Figure 3.9 of the number of strikers.

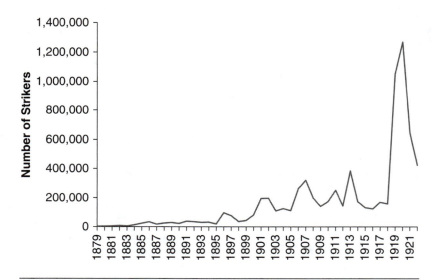

Figure 3.9 The Period From 1919 to 1922 in Historical Perspective (Plot of Number of Strikers, 1879–1921)

Yet whereas the years between 1919 and 1920 saw an unprecedented upsurge in working-class mobilization (the "red years," or *biennio rosso*), the subsequent 2 years witnessed a bloody reaction by the hands of the fascists (the "black years," or *biennio nero*). It all ended in October 1922 with Mussolini's takeover of power and 20 years of fascist dictatorship.

There are good historical and theoretical reasons to study that period: (1) Fascism, along with communism and democracy, represents one of the three roads to the modern world (in Barrington Moore's (1966) rendering); (2) Italy was the first country to open the fascist road, coining the very term *fascism*; in just 4 years, Italy went from a revolutionary situation on the left to a revolution on the right, from mobilization to countermobilization; and (3) there is no agreed-on theory of fascism, different scholars viewing fascism as the result of the behavior of different social actors:

- Class alliance between state, landed elite, industrial bourgeoisie (Moore, 1966)
- Class alliance between state and landed elite (Rueschemeyer, Stephens, & Stephens, 1992)
- Class alliance between industrial bourgeoisie and petty bourgeoisie (Poulantzas, 1970)
- Reaction to socialism by petty bourgeoisie (Lipset, 1959)
- Reaction to socialism by industrial bourgeoisie (Lenin, Third Communist International; see De Felice, 1969, pp. 63–69)

To study those years, I coded data from three newspapers, *Il Lavoro, Avanti!* (the official paper of the Socialist Party), and *Popolo d'Italia* (the official paper of the Fascist Party). Here, I focus on the *Avanti!* data (18,000 articles yielding some 140,000 semantic triplets).

Let's run some simple queries on the *Avanti!* database to find answers to questions about the period from 1919 to 1922. I rely on the PC-ACE query manager, rather than SQL, for these queries. The query manager was designed as a GUI (graphical user interface) to allow even users with no knowledge of SQL and relational database systems to perform queries. The GUI translates a query based on the objects of a user-defined story grammar (and known to the user) into an SQL query based on the underlying PC-ACE tables and fields (which are unknown to the user, since the table structure is controlled directly by the program). Let's start with a query to obtain a list of the collective actors stored in the database (Figure 3.10).

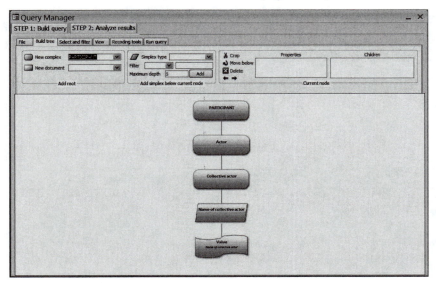

Figure 3.10   PC-ACE Query Manager: Querying for Participants/Actors

The query yields the list of available records (Figure 3.11).

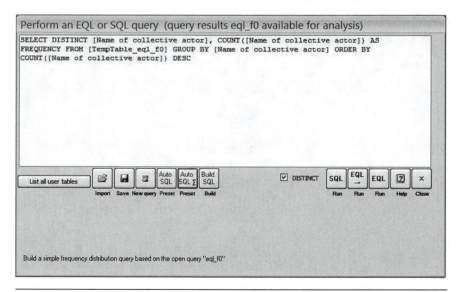

Figure 3.11 PC-ACE Query Manager: Query Results (List of Actors)

The SQL query button shown in Figure 3.11 would then allow you to compute a frequency distribution automatically (Figure 3.12).[13]

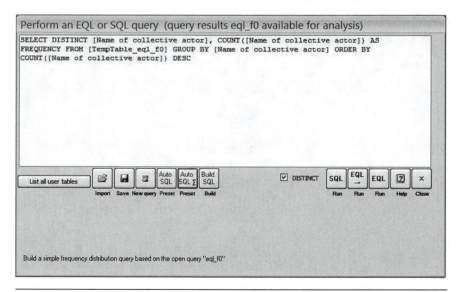

Figure 3.12 PC-ACE Query Manager (SQL Builder)

Running the query as an SQL query would then yield the frequency distribution of the actors present in the database (Figure 3.13).

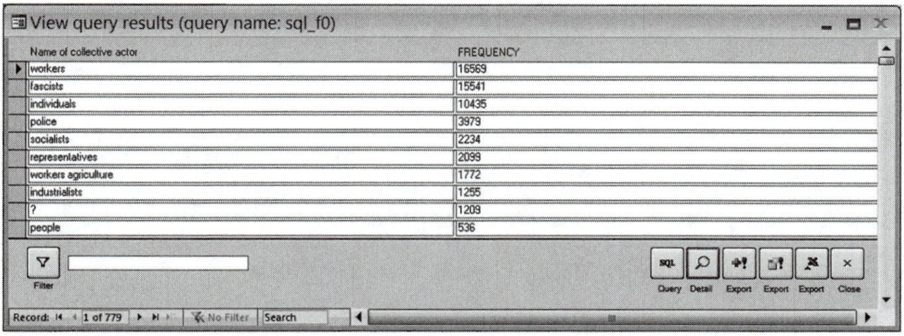

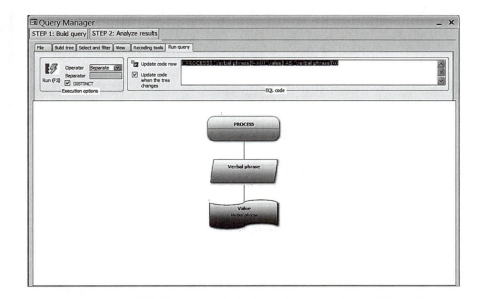

Figure 3.13 PC-ACE Query Manager: Query Results (Frequency of Actors)

From workers (including workers in agriculture) and socialists to fascists, industrialists, and police, the frequency distribution of actors confirms the stuff that periods of high mobilization are made of: varied numbers of social actors jostling for positions. Similarly, the query of processes (Figure 3.14) yields the frequency distribution of actions (Figure 3.15).

Figure 3.14 PC-ACE Query Manager: Querying for Processes/Actions

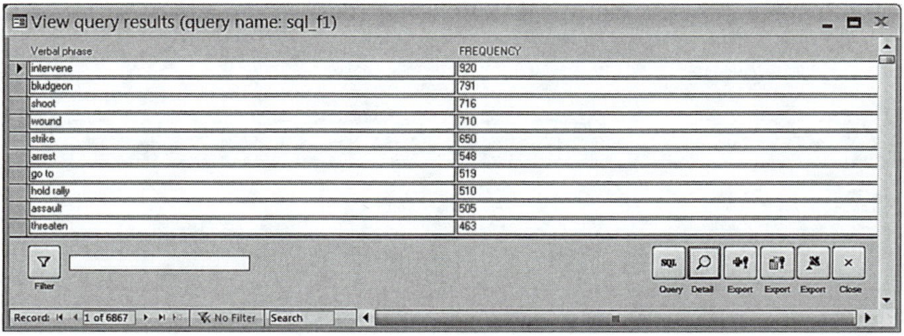

80

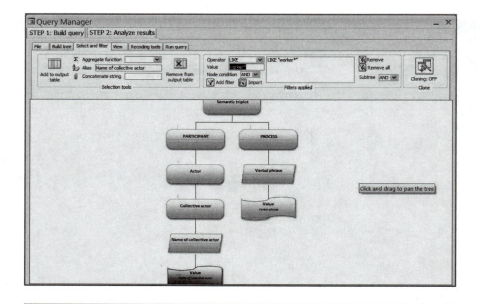

Figure 3.15   PC-ACE Query Manager: Query Results (Actions)

Again, the frequency of actions attests to the turbulent nature of those years, with a great deal of collective actions (e.g., strike, rally) and violence (e.g., bludgeon, shoot, assault). But who was involved in the violence? Was it the workers, the socialists, the fascists? Who did what in those turbulent years? To answer these questions, we need to run a query that computes the frequency distributions of the actions committed by the various actors. For workers, the query shown in Figure 3.16 ultimately yields the results shown in Figure 3.17.

Figure 3.16   PC-ACE Query Manager: Querying for Workers and Their Actions

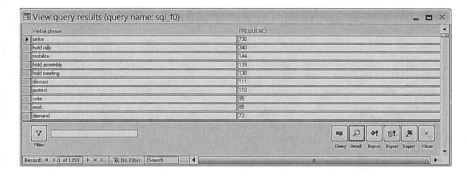

Figure 3.17   PC-ACE Query Manager: Query Results (Workers and Their Actions)

There is no indication from these data of systematic use of violence by workers (although there are a handful of workers' violent actions among the less frequent actions). What about the fascists? Which actions were they involved in? The query results of Figure 3.18 show that it was indeed the fascists who were involved in much of the violence of those years.

The combined results of Figures 3.17 and 3.18 clearly show the surge in working class mobilization of the red years and the demobilization and countermobilization by the fascists of the black years.

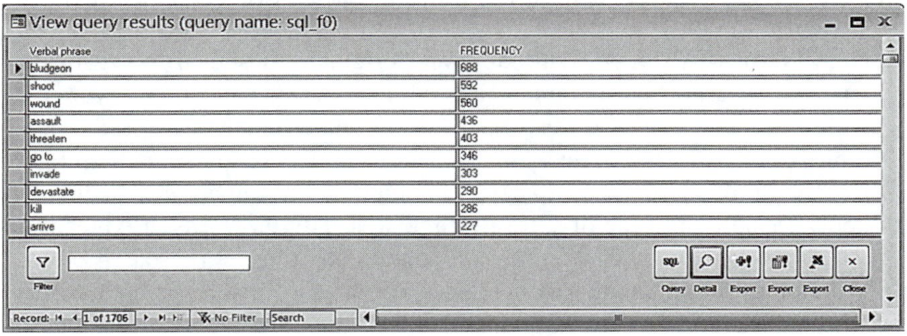

Figure 3.18   PC-ACE Query Manager: Query Results (Fascists and Their Actions)

The Trick Behind Numbers

In the end, the trick behind the alchemic transformation of words into numbers is quite simple: You count. And having the different types of information conveniently separated into appropriate categories (actors in the actor category, actions in the action category, time in the time category, etc.), all related to one another, makes counting easier. It also makes it possible to find answers to questions such as the following: Which actors (or types of actors) perform given actions? Whom did the fascists clash with in 1921? What kinds of actions did women perform during the mobilization of 1919? Indeed, it is the relational properties of PC-ACE data structure (or of any RDBMS) that makes possible the statistical analysis of what are basically words, despite the complexity of the structure. We will see in the next chapter what kind of statistical analyses you can do on the thousands of words structured within the categories of a story grammar and stored in an RDBMS.

Notice: when working with different hierarchical levels (e.g., dispute, subdispute, event, semantic triplet), be aware that the numbers you get will vary depending on the level of aggregation you chose to work with. Those numbers will typically be higher if you count individual occurrences of objects (e.g., actors or actions) and progressively lower if you count triplets, events, or disputes (unless each of these objects occurs with a frequency of 1).

Software Design Matters: CAQDAS Versus PC-ACE

Software design does not happen in a vacuum. It is meant to meet certain needs, and, if well designed, a software package will optimally satisfy those needs. Qualitative data analysis software packages (e.g., ATLAS.ti, N6, NVivo, MAXQDA, WinMax) were originally designed to organize pages of field notes or the transcripts of open-ended, in-depth interviews: researchers could mark different portions of text as belonging to different topics of interest (assigning them to selected "codes") and then pull up for inspection all the portions of text belonging to the same code. In time, oddly enough, this type of software came to satisfy the needs of typically quantitative researchers who rely on content analysis as a research tool. With topics simply thought of as themes, it is an easy step to thematic content analysis, with its frequencies of various themes and cross-correlations. But whether used for qualitative or quantitative purposes, the basic principle of the design of this type of qualitative data analysis software is a linear, seriatim organization of codes, much like traditional thematic content analysis.

In contrast to qualitative data analysis software, PC-ACE was designed to meet the needs of quantitative narrative analysis, with applications in sociohistorical research based on archival documents or newspapers. It was designed to find answers to questions for/from a story: What did a specific instance of an actor do? For example, which actions did the actor "fascist" do? And if the action was one of violence, let's say "knock down," what did they knock down? Who was the target of their violence? Was it the socialists? Where did the violence by fascists against socialists occur?

These different needs led to different designs in both data entry (coding) and data query.

Data Entry (Coding)

All qualitative data analysis software (CAQDAS) expect documents to be imported into the software. Coding is done by highlighting a portion of a document text and assigning it to a code selected from a list. In the current release of PC-ACE, documents reside in an external medium (e.g., a book or a microfilm), and coders use combo boxes and text boxes to enter text of interest in appropriate coding categories (Figure 3.19).

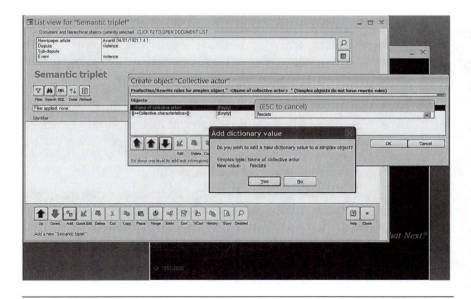

Figure 3.19   Data Entry (Coding) in PC-ACE

There are, of course, great advantages to having the original texts at your fingertips, a click away from your coded output. But for documents that are not in machine-readable form, there are some drawbacks: You will need to get your text into a digitized file, first; and this can be a lengthy and time-consuming process.

The Golden Rules of QNA Coding

Rule Number 1: Code one textual item per coding category. This does not necessarily mean one word per category (the story grammar is a semantic structure, not syntactical); but certainly one meaningful textual item per category (e.g., knock down) (if you use software such as MAXQDA or ATLAS.ti, you may actually need to code an entire sentence).

Rule Number 2: As an extension of the previous rule, put the right textual item in the right category (e.g., a city in space and not time).

Rule Number 3: Use the wording found in the original documents (i.e., do not change "tradesmen" to "workers"). Of course, this recommendation does not apply if you use software such as MAXQDA or ATLAS.ti, where a portion of the original text (whether sentence, paragraph, or other) becomes part of the code and cannot be changed.

Rule Number 4: As an extension of the previous rule, do not aggregate information during data entry (original disaggregated information cannot be retrieved from aggregated data). As Markoff et al. (1975) argued, "The coder transcribes a set of symbols which are intended to be as close as possible to the level of concreteness in the original document . . . The coder translates; the scientist analyzes" (p. 41). Although the coder never quite "translates" (a translation is never neutral, never gives back an exact copy of the original), Markoff et al. are correct in insisting that the code should be as close as possible to the original, indeed be based on the very same text expressions of the original.

Rule Number 5: Turn passive sentences into active ones (when the subject is really unknown, perhaps code it with a question mark, ?). Alternatively, code the semantic role of subject and object to disambiguate between agents and patients, messenger and recipient (Franzosi, 2004b, pp. 122–124).

Rule Number 6: Convert grammatical subjects in a clause such as "they" or "who" to the real subject (e.g., rewrite the clauses in the *Avanti!* article "they tore down a wall and once inside they destroyed all the furniture and various portraits" as "the fascists tore down a wall and once inside the fascists destroyed all the furniture and various portraits").

Rule Number 7: Convert gerundive verbs into proper clauses. For example, the paragraph (emphasis added) "A group of fascists, *crossing* the city walls . . . knocked down the entrance door . . . *breaking* all the furniture and *removing* documents" would have to be rewritten as "A group of fascists crossed the city walls . . . knocked down the entrance door . . . broke all the furniture and removed documents."

Rule Number 8: Order your coded sentences (the semantic triplets) chronologically. In the study of events, you are interested in the story rather than the plot (although the plot is an important aspect of how the story is told, of the ideological production of the documents you use as sources).

Rule Number 9: Last but not least, focus on the purely narrative passages of your text; code the narrative clauses and sentences only, skipping description and evaluation; these aspects of narrative do not conform to the linguistic structure of a story grammar, and coding this type of information within the categories of a story grammar would be cumbersome, time-consuming, and unreliable.

A point to remember: to repeat a point already made, you do not need to code thousands of documents if your sole interest is in plot rather than story (Rule Number 8), in description and evaluation rather than action (Rule Number 9). But if you do want to code description and evaluation, then these golden rules of QNA coding would require some tweaking. Rule Number 9 would be the first one to go: If evaluation and description are important to you, you cannot focus on purely narrative elements only. Rules Number 5 and 8 would probably have to follow the fate of Rule Number 9. Given the ideological valence of passive syntactical constructs (a form of evaluation), you may not wish to turn passive forms into active ones (Rule Number 5). Similarly, the sequential order of narrative elements (descriptive, evaluative, or purely narrative) will reflect not only the respondents' storytelling skills but also their feelings about the relative importance of different discourse parts (as reflected by a need to foreground and background, story vs. plot) (Rule Number 8).

Questions (and Answers) About Coding (Units of Analysis)

Question

When you are confronted with a document, how much text do you read before starting to code? Do you read the entire document, a paragraph, a sentence?

Answer

In content analysis, these issues are known under the general heading of "unitizing" (or of units of analysis, see Krippendorf, 1980, pp. 57–63), with at least the three following different types of units.

- *Sampling unit:* The individual document that is sampled to be content analyzed (e.g., a newspaper article on lynching or on fascism)
- *Recording unit:* The specific text that is assigned to a single coding category (e.g., the expression "knock down," rather than just "knock")
- *Context unit:* The amount of text within which to look for the occurrence of a specific coding category (e.g., a sentence, a paragraph, or even the entire document).

Your question deals specifically with the "context unit." Since in QNA the "semantic triplet" holds together a number of more basic recording units (e.g., an actor, an action, a city), you need to read as much text from your sampling unit as to be able to form a proper semantic triplet (e.g., skipping description or evaluation). At that point, you start coding all "qualifying" information (i.e., information that fits the categories of your semantic triplet).

Question

When you have different documents describing the same event or dispute, if you code everything from every document, don't you risk duplicating some information? Isn't this dangerous in historical research as you may end up with two World Wars II (and one was bad enough)?

Answer

Indeed. If you are using documents to study action rather than discourse (e.g., in historical research), to avoid the problem of duplicating historical events, you code any "qualifying" information as soon as you encounter it in a document (on a "first come, first serve" basis, so to speak). From then on, you skip any duplicated information provided within the same document or across different documents. From any given document, *you only code new information placing it in the appropriate coding category of the appropriate semantic triplet* (even if all you end up coding from a document is just the <number>; e.g., "thousands of workers struck today in Peru," where the information about the workers' strike has already been given in other documents but the number of participants—"thousands"—is new information). Context units need not be contiguous.

Question

What do you do if different documents provide different and perhaps even contradictory accounts of the same event?

Answer

If different documents provide the same information on an event, you just cross-reference the event to all the documents with repeated information (i.e., you link the event to the set of documents that provide repeated information). If, on the other hand, some documents say one thing and others say another thing, you can use rewrite rules to make that contradiction explicit for any object of your grammar (e.g., dispute, event, semantic triplet). For example, in the following rewrite rules, the <dispute> can be rewritten as a set of events and of alternative events that provide a different account of what happened:

<dispute>   →   {<event> [<alternative event>]}

<alternative event>   →   <event>

Coding categories that are typically subject to disputed claims according to the source, for example, the <number of participants> of an event, can be rewritten in the following way:

<number of participants>   →   <number> [<source of information>]

Where the number varies with the <source of information>,

<source of information>   →   police | union | party | organizers | . . .

Question
What if you are not entirely sure of the meaning of a text and, as a result, you are not sure how to code it?

Answer
Again, you can use the rewrite rules to build that uncertainty into your coding scheme. The following rewrite rules would accomplish just that:

<event>   →   {<semantic triplet> [<level of certainty>]}

<level of certainty>   →   <percent> [<reason>]

<percent>   →   10% | 20% | . . . 100%

<reason>   →   document unreadable | poorly written | . . .

Data Query

To be able to perform a query that allows you to answer questions for/from a story as required by QNA, two things are necessary in ATLAS.ti (but also N6, NVivo, MAXQDA, and WinMax, which work in similar ways). First, the codes for actors or actions (or any object of the grammar for that matter, as shown in Figure 3.3) must include, as part of the code label, the specific values that the object takes on (e.g., for actor and action, the codes are Participant_Actor_Fascists, Participant_Actor_Police, Process_Verb_break,

Process_Verb_destroy). Second, different codes must be assigned repeatedly to the same portion of text (e.g., Process_Verb_Knock_down and Partici-pant_Object_Physical Object_entrance door). With some 1,600 distinct values for actors in the *Avanti!* database (and 7,000 distinct entries for actions), this would lead to a bewildering number of codes, making the process of data coding quite cumbersome.

In PC-ACE (or any RDBMS based on SQL), the codes (or objects of the story grammar) are separate from their values. Specific values of a code (*column* in RDMS jargon or object of a story grammar) would be specified in the *where* statement of an SQL query. As a result, doing QNA in ATLAS.ti (or any of the qualitative data analysis software) would work best by using only a handful of highly aggregated codes. More problematically, ATLAS.ti queries pull up records of quotes but not matrices of cooccur-rences, vital numbers for any data analysis. Query results would have to be manipulated further in SPSS (where, for instance, you can export data from ATLAS.ti).

Exporting Data for Statistical Analyses

Statistical data analyses (of the type we review in the next chapter) require data in numeric format. Different software will make it more or less easy for you to get those numbers. In ATLAS.ti (as in all CAQDAS pro-grams) and PC-ACE, data export is the result of query operations.

ATLAS.ti queries will list all quotations requested in the query and pro-vide a frequency count. Beyond that single number, however, you would need to export your codes to SPSS for further manipulation. ATLAS.ti is intended primarily for supporting qualitative reasoning processes. As the ATLAS.ti manual states,

> Especially with large amounts of data, it is sometimes useful to analyze the data in a quantitative manner using statistical approaches. ATLAS.ti pro-vides an export function to permit further processing of the syntax file by SPSS®, the Statistical Package for the Social Sciences. (Muhr & Friese, 2004, p. 299)

For network matrices, you would need to compute the frequency for each relation and fill in by hand the values of each cell of a network matrix (see Figure 4.4), quite a time-consuming process for large matrices.

Like ATLAS.ti, PC-ACE does not have any statistical capabilities; but SQL queries based on the *count* statement do allow you to compute fre-quencies and frequency distributions in very general ways (i.e., sets of numbers rather than single numbers). These SQL query results can then be exported to an Excel spreadsheet (or to a database table; see Figures 3.13, 3.15, 3.17, or 3.18) for import into specialized software for further data analysis (e.g., UCINET or Pajek for network analysis or ARCGIS or GRASS for spatial analyses). PC-ACE also computes automatically network matrices (and for different temporal frequencies, daily, weekly, monthly, quarterly, yearly, or for selected periods); they can be imported or cut and pasted directly into UCINET or other network programs.

A Focus on PC-ACE

Data Verification

For as long as coding must be done by humans, coding is subject to errors, no matter how sophisticated your data entry software is in trapping them.[14] That being the case, don't forget to allocate a good chunk of your budget (if lucky; otherwise, of your time) for data verification. Remember this: The quality of your inferences will only be as good as the quality of your evidence. ATLAS.ti, MAXQDA, and similar software display original text and coded output side by side, making it easy to verify the output (but, unfortunately, only to a limited extent can coding schemes designed in this software resemble a story grammar). In PC-ACE, the original documents are not imported directly into the software.[15] PC-ACE, however, exploits properties of narrative to help improve the quality of coded output: semantic coherence.

Semantic Coherence

Working with a linguistic approach to content analysis (i.e., with a story grammar as your coding scheme) has a great advantage: By preserving in coded output the structural properties of narrative, error detection is much easier (and more natural). Like the original input narrative text, coded output must be semantically coherent. It must make sense to any "competent user of the language." The various objects coded within a semantic triplet must be meaningfully related to one another (local coherence). In turn, the semantic triplets within an event must also be in a meaningful sequential order and must be in meaningful relation to one or more dominant themes or topics appearing in the text as a whole (global coherence). At both the intratriplet level and across triplets, coded output is coherent if it squares with the reader's understanding of real-life activities. A "competent" reader should recognize as errors intrasentence semantic violations (e.g., "workers lay off employer"). Ideally, software designed for quantitative narrative analysis should display all coded output in narrative form, with coded information organized around the SAO structure in proper sequential order.[16] Even a quick glance at coded output displayed in narrative form would allow a reader to gauge intrasentence and intersentence coherence (see Figure 3.20 for PC-ACE narrative display of coded output).[17]

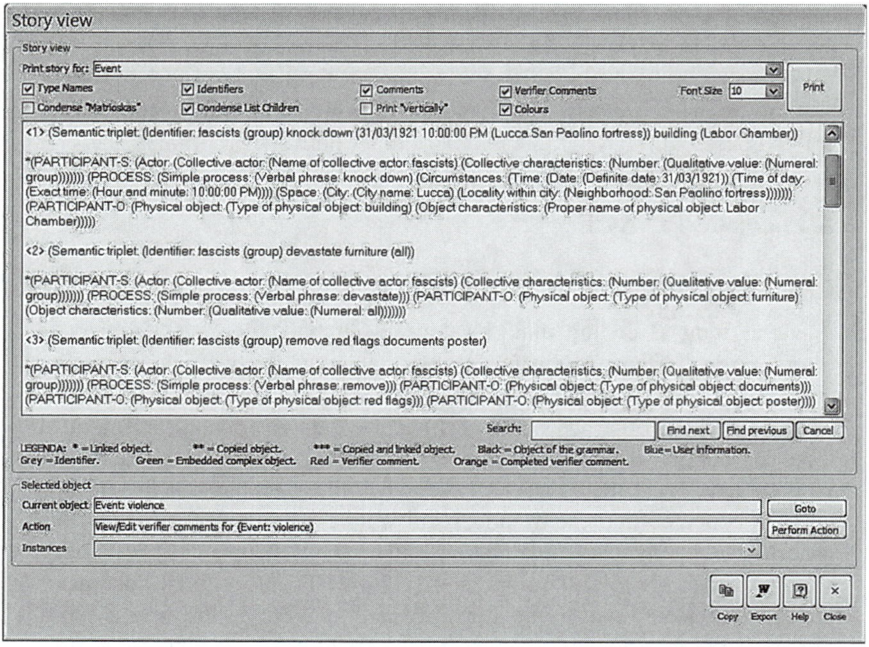

Figure 3.20 PC-ACE Narrative Display of Coded Output

Checking Output Against Input

Verification for semantic coherence, no doubt, provides a powerful tool for checking the accuracy of coded information either directly by the coder or, at a later stage, by an independent verifier. Yet this type of data verification only guarantees general readability and acceptability of output; it does not guarantee correspondence between input (source) and output (code). Output can make perfect sense but be the product of a coder's imagination. To catch this type of error would require a different type of output verification: direct comparison of the coded output with the original source material (input vs. output verification). Verification should be carried out with an eye for both document omission and accuracy of information entered.

Data Cleaning

Data verification, either concurrent with data collection or during the early stages of data analysis, will no doubt turn up several types of coding errors that need to be corrected (a process known as "data cleaning"):

1. The simplest type of error is misspellings (e.g., "striike" instead of "strike").

2. A second type of error is text placed in the wrong category (e.g., "male" coded under <type of actor> rather than <sex>).

3. A third type of error is having similar expressions coded in different coding categories (e.g., "blue-collar workers" may have been coded as: <subject> ("workers") plus the modifier <type> ("blue-collar") or as <subject> ("workers") plus the modifier <occupation> ("blue-collar"). This is not a serious problem if you are aware that you can find certain items of information in different categories. You can then write SQL SELECT statements that look up the information in different tables. But the larger the number of tables you need to access for information, the slower a query.

4. A fourth type of error is coding too many (and different) things in the same coding category (e.g., "blue-collar and white-collar workers" all under <subject>). Use the frequency distribution of the number of words contained in a coding category as a gauge of this type of error. A high number of words in a category may betray coding errors. Make sure to compute and inspect this simple indicator.

For all these errors, SQL provides powerful tools for data cleaning.

Let SQL Do the Work for You

SQL is a powerful tool not only for data querying, for asking questions about stories coded in a relational database via *select* statements. It can also be very useful after data coding, for the purpose of data cleaning and data aggregation via *insert into* and *update* statements. The syntax of these statements is similar to that of the *select* statement used for a regular search query:

Insert Into table_name

Values (value1, value2,. . . .)

The SQL *insert* statements allow you to add rows to a table (e.g., adding an explicit object). You can even combine *select* and *insert into* statements to specify conditions for the creation of new objects. You can also update values in existing records via the *update* statement:

Update table_name

set column_name = new_value

where column_name = some_value

Thus, in the dictionary_table of our sample database, we could change the values "entrance door" and "internal side doors" to "door"

Update dictionary_table

set Value = "door"

where Value = "entrance door" *or* Value = "internal side doors"

Via the *insert into* and *update* statements, you can use SQL to do some of the most repetitive coding work for you. For instance, you could impute time and space automatically to every action or triplet within an event if you code this information only at the event level (but it would be then required at the action level by an SQL query designed to extract spatiotemporal information at the triplet level).

SQL update queries would be particularly useful for automatically recoding certain types of intercoder discrepancies, for example, when different coders assign the same textual element to different coding categories (e.g., a coder assigning "blue-collar" to the coding category <type of actor> and another coder assigning it to <occupation>). Don't worry too much about this type of breakdown in intercoder reliability. A frequency distribution of textual elements by coding category would easily reveal this type of discrepancy, and an update query would move all instances of a textual element (e.g., "blue-collar") from one category to another.

Data Aggregation

A simple frequency distribution of actors and actions in the *Avanti!* PC-ACE database yields 1,600 distinct entries for actors and 7,000 for actions (out of some 140,000 semantic triplets, i.e., skeleton narrative sentences). Such a large number of different values is altogether typical for this kind of research (e.g., Ericsson & Simon, 1996, pp. 265–266; Tilly, 1995, pp. 414–415); but typical or not, it poses serious problems when it comes to data analysis. We need to aggregate these values into a more manageable set of aggregated categories.

Linguists refer to this process of aggregation as linguistic categorization (Labov, 1973; Taylor, 2004). Taylor makes it clear that linguistic categorization occurs at multiple levels. Words can be categorized as nouns or verbs (or participants and processes, in terms of our story grammar). But a social scientist may further categorize participants into different types of participants (e.g., social groups or physical objects), and social groups into different types of social groups (e.g., workers, employers, political parties, state), depending on different underlying categorization criteria. Similarly, processes (or the distinct verbs that make up processes) can belong to different spheres of action (e.g., violence, conflict, bargaining, play, emotions). Thus, actions such as "go" and "get in" in the dictionary_table (see Table 3.5) may be conveniently grouped together under an aggregate sphere of action labeled "movement," while "knock down," "break," "remove," "tear down" and "destroy" belong to "violence."

And More Work for SQL

SQL update queries can be conveniently used to carry out data aggregation of this kind in a semi-automatic mode. Consider the action_table of our sample database (Table 3.3); let's add a new column to that table, aggregate_code (Table 3.6). The following two SQL UPDATE queries will automatically generate the aggregated codes for actions with the results as given in Table 3.6.

Update action_table *set* aggregate_code = "violence"

where dictionary_value = "knock down"

Table 3.6   action_table of Sample RDBMS Modified for Aggregate Codes

ID	triplet_ID	dictionary_ID	aggregate_code
1	1	2	Movement
2	2	3	Violence
3	3	6	Violence
4	4	8	Violence
5	5	2	Movement
6	6	12	Movement
7	7	13	Violence

or dictionary_value = "break"

or dictionary_value = "remove"

or dictionary_value = "tear down"

or dictionary_value = "destroy"

Update action_table *set* aggregate_code = "movement"

where dictionary_value = "go"

or dictionary_value = "get in"

You could also decide to work at different levels of aggregations, distinguishing between violence against things and violence against people. Thus, "break down" and "destroy" would be aggregated as "violence against things," whereas verbs such as "wound" or "kill" would be aggregated as "violence against people." The aggregate codes "violence against things" and "violence against people" could then be further aggregated into a single aggregate code, "violence."

In PC-ACE, the SQL work of data cleaning and data aggregation based on insert and update clauses is made easier by a GUI, the Update Manager, similar to the Query Manager. The Update Manager allows users with no background in database design and SQL to work with the objects of their story grammar rather than with PC-ACE tables as required by SQL clauses. The Update Manager converts the GUI objects into an SQL query that it will execute in the background.

Problems With Automatic Aggregation:
One More Golden Rule of QNA Coding

SQL can help you with data cleaning and data aggregation, doing much of the work for you semi-automatically, via insert and update statements carried out *after* the completion of data collection. Unfortunately, SQL batch update queries potentially run into problems with words with multiple (and/or even contradictory) meanings. It is the context that gives a word its specific meaning: "Shout" could be a verb of verbal violence, a verb of symbolic actions (such as singing), or a defensive verb (shouting out of fear). Such disambiguation would require accessing the original source document, a time-consuming task (one would have to locate the document if documents have not been brought into the software itself, and, in any case, the document would have to be reread).

To avoid costly solutions to data aggregation problems, when aggregation is carried out *after* data collection, you may wish to consider having the coder carry out *both* data coding (in highly disaggregated form) and data aggregation at the same time. Rewrite rules can help you formalize this approach, using two separate coding categories instead of one. Take the <process>, which had the following rewrite rule:

<process>   →   <verb> [<negation>][<modality>]
                  <circumstances>

A new category (e.g., <aggregated verb code>) would need to be added to the rewrite rule:

<process>   →   <verb> <aggregated verb code>
                  [<negation>][<modality>]
                  <circumstances>

This way, the verb "kill" would be coded as such in the category <verb> and as "violence" in the category <aggregated verb code> during data entry. This suggests an additional coding rule to the list provided earlier, a corollary to Rule Number 4 ("do not aggregate information during data entry"):

Rule Number 10: Carry out *both* data coding, in the wording of the original document, and data aggregation during data entry/data collection (but *never* data aggregation by itself).

Reliance on such a rule will save you precious time during the phase of data aggregation since you will not need to access original documents to disambiguate meaning. Of course, depending on the design of aggregate categories, the coder may come to play "surrogate scientist." Aggregate categories based on "natural" linguistic principles (e.g., verbs such as *kick, wound, beat up, kill,* and *bludgeon* aggregated into a sphere of action of violence) will be more reliable than categories based on abstract and theoretical principles (stay away from these!). Unfortunately, this is the risk you run when carrying out QNA in CAQDAS programs. In this type of software, to not multiply codes to a bewildering number and make the process of coding unwieldy, you have no choice but to work with a manageable list of highly aggregated codes. If you are not relying on CAQDAS programs for your QNA application, you can minimize the risk of the "surrogate scientist" problem by treating aggregate codes as temporary codes (subject to further inspection and validation no differently from disaggregated codes).

Fuzzy Meaning, Fuzzy Sets

Working with mutually exclusive categories has great appeal in problems of taxonomy: It avoids the ambiguities of multiple- and cross-classification; it makes it easier to search for occurrences of items, by having to look in one category only. Not surprisingly, early developers

96

of content analysis recommended coding scheme designs based on exhaustive and mutually exclusive categories—a recommendation embraced by later developers and users (e.g., Leites & de Sola Pool, 1942/2008, pp. 145–148; Holsti, 1969, pp. 95, 99–100; on these issues, see Franzosi, 2008, p. xxvii).

Indeed, if the boundaries between the categories of a classification system are clear, the principle of mutual exclusion in classification certainly works well. Yet taxonomies are rarely based on such clearly defined, separate categories. Colors come in such a great variety of hues that to sort all of them into a small set of primary or even secondary colors may be problematic. And when it comes to words, their classification into neatly defined and separate categories is even more problematic. Words simply have too many (or too fuzzy) meanings to fall neatly into mutually exclusive categories.

For Propp (1928/1968), "identical acts can have different meanings— Functions (actions) can not be distributed around mutually exclusive axes" (p. 21). Austin (1962/1975, p. 150; see also Levin, 1993, p. 18), in his *How to Do Things With Words,* similarly proposed "more general families of related and overlapping speech acts," rather than a system of mutually exclusive classes. The vagueness of linguistic boundaries compels Labov (1973, p. 343) to write, in a seminal work on categorization, "linguistics . . . becomes a form of boundary theory rather than a category theory." Halliday's (1985/1994, p. 107) classification of processes acknowledges the fluidity of boundaries between process categories, each category "sharing some features of each" adjacent category.

Beware of the limits of exhaustiveness and mutual exclusion of categories when aggregating words. Build the fuzziness of meaning into your aggregate codes, using multiple codes for all instances of fuzzy meanings. Thus, the action "remove" of our *Avanti!* story could be aggregated as both an action of movement and an action of violence. Fuzzy meaning requires fuzzy logic and fuzzy sets (as represented by multiple overlapping circles rather than disjoint circles) (on the general problem of using fuzzy logic and fuzzy sets in the social sciences, see Ragin, 2000, 2008).

Question and Answer (Which Software Should I Use?)

Question
Granted, "No software, no QNA." But there is typically a steep learning curve for new software. Which software would you recommend for QNA?

Answer

The answer to that question depends on several factors. Here are some for you to consider.

1. Whether you wish to code only the purely narrative clauses found in your documents via a story grammar or whether you also wish to code other parts of those texts that do not fit easily into the categories of a story grammar. CAQDAS programs are ideally suited for "thematic" coding and have a harder time with complex story grammars. PC-ACE can cope with either thematic or narrative approaches.

2. The average portion of purely narrative text across all the documents under investigation. If the amount of narrative proper (action) to be coded is minimal and you do not use a fully blown story grammar as your coding scheme, then CAQDAS programs would work.

3. The complexity of the story grammar you wish to adopt. CAQDAS programs do not allow you to implement complex story grammars, whereas PC-ACE was designed for a story grammar approach to text coding.

4. Whether the documents to be analyzed are already in digital form (e.g., Word, ASCII) or can be easily converted into digital form. CAQDAS programs expect documents to be available in the programs themselves; PC-ACE does not. For some types of documents (e.g., handwritten, microfilmed) the cost of converting the documents may be high. By the time you have converted the documents . . . you could have coded them.

5. The amount of material to be coded. In very large projects, based on thousands of documents, PC-ACE is a must, given its ability to extract numbers from words (e.g., automatic computation of network matrices) by manipulating data in very general forms through SQL. In small projects, the limited capabilities of data manipulation in CAQDAS programs, that is, the extra steps of having to export codes to SPSS for further manipulation to perform statistical analyses, are not such a heavy burden.

6. Available resources: Some of these software programs are free (AutoMap, PC-ACE); others need to be purchased (e.g., CAQDAS programs), unless you work in institutions with site licenses.

7. General and local know-how about a given software program. With most software, it is easy to get started, but advanced options often require heavy investments of time. Having people around (physically or ideally in Web-based user groups) who can provide help when you are stuck is always convenient. Specialized research software (e.g., AutoMap or PC-ACE) have small user groups. Commercial CAQDAS programs are very popular, with diffused knowledge about their use (and they all work in similar ways). If you work in an institution that supports a specific package, there will typically be a great deal of local know-how (and perhaps even institutional IT software support).

In sum, I would strongly recommend using PC-ACE for large-scale sociohistorical research focused on story grammars (e.g., in the tradition of protest event analysis). I would also recommend using PC-ACE for projects where coding categories are linked to one another in complex, hierarchical, and relational ways and where the aim is to produce quantitative analyses.

A Note on the Organization of Coding

It is tempting, particularly when the documents you are analyzing are stored in the computer along with your QNA software, to code the relevant bits of information into the categories of your story grammar, one document after the other, in the "natural" order of appearance of these documents (the document key, sorted by specific objects of the key; e.g., date, title, page for newspaper articles; the story title, author, publication date, publisher, and page for a children's story). If each document narrates a different dispute/ macro-event/story (dispute, for simplicity), this strategy makes perfect sense. It maximizes both efficiency and reliability: You read each document once, and you code all the necessary information with no interferences from other stories (one-pass coding).

But take a different scenario: A dispute is narrated across different documents. If you code documents in their natural order, rather than *within* each dispute, you will jump from one dispute to another, back and forth across disputes. No doubt, your brain will soon experience information overload. The work by cognitive psychologists on text understanding and recall (on the basis of story grammars) shows that people take more time and make more errors when reading, comprehending, and recalling stories where important elements of a story are missing or scrambled (particularly with elements taken from other stories), independent of story length (Mandler, 1982; Mandler & Johnson, 1977; Stein, 1982a, 1982b; Stein & Glenn, 1979; Stein & Policastro, 1984). Most likely, reliability (and even efficiency, coding taking longer than expected) will suffer.

A better strategy would be based on two-pass (or even multiple-pass) coding. In the first pass, you collate documents into disputes, providing a general title for each dispute. In the second pass, you code each dispute separately, dealing only with the documents of that particular dispute. In two-pass coding, you focus on one story at a time, from beginning to end without time lapses or interference from other intervening stories. This uninterrupted focus greatly reduces the risk of duplicating events, facilitates reliable chronological ordering of information, and helps detect inconsistencies in the information found in different documents on the same event.

Take yet another scenario: Not only are stories/events typically narrated across a number of documents, but each document also talks about different and unrelated stories/events. The two-pass coding strategy of focusing on one story at a time, jumping from one document to the next within the same story, with an eye to maximizing reliability, may run into serious efficiency problems. You may end up having to read some documents several times, as many times, in fact, as the number of different stories found in the set of multiple-story documents. Thus, two-pass coding increases data reliability in the presence of multiple-document disputes but decreases efficiency in the presence of multiple-dispute documents.

Only a clear understanding of the nature of your documents will allow you to make the right decision on how to organize the coding task, striking the right balance between reliability and efficiency. In my 1920 *Il Lavoro* newspaper data, more than 98% of the articles deal with only one dispute. The corresponding figure for a 1972 newspaper, *Unità,* is 78%. In absolute figures, only 75 articles covered more than one dispute in 1920, compared with 1,865 such articles in 1972. These differences in reporting practices can greatly affect data collection costs. So know your documents (but don't forget your coder, either)!

Notice: CAQDAS computer programs (e.g., ATLAS.ti) allow you to organize documents into "families," that is, into groups of documents linked together by some organizing principle (e.g., they all talk about the same event). PC-ACE similarly allows you to cross-reference different documents to the same hierarchical object (e.g., dispute). And with both types of software, the same document can be assigned to more than one family or can be cross-referenced to several hierarchical objects. Use families or cross-referenced hierarchical complex objects and then code sequentially each document within a specific family or hierarchical complex object.

Coding and Aggregating: Some Recommendations

The efficient and reliable organization of the coding task involves yet another choice. Of the various tasks involved in QNA (data entry or coding, data verification, data cleaning, data aggregation, and data analysis), it may be tempting to have coders carry out both data coding and data aggregation at the same time during data entry (that is true even if *you* are the sole coder, as in most dissertation projects); it may perhaps be even more tempting to carry out coding on the basis of highly aggregated codes. Why bother with disaggregated codes if, in the end, you need to work with aggregated codes during data analysis? After all, as Koopmans and Statham (1999) write, "to some extent [data aggregation] constitutes a second coding of the coding" (p. 208). Here are my recommendations:

1. Work at a disaggregated level, using the very words found in the original documents (something easily done in CAQDAS programs or in software programs where documents are imported into the software, where parts of the text are marked as belonging to a particular code).

2. You can always aggregate disaggregated data, but you cannot disaggregate aggregated data without going back to the original (and this can be a VERY time-consuming process, particularly when compared with the time needed for aggregating disaggregated codes; it took me several long years using teams of coders to code the *Avanti!* data but only a few weeks for aggregating the codes).

3. Avoid highly aggregated codes based on theoretical principles. This approach risks turning coders into "surrogate scientists" (Markoff et al., 1975, p. 37). Unfortunately, this is a choice you may not have with CAQDAS programs since the alternative would lead to an unwieldy proliferation of code.

4. When you rely on RDBMS-based software (yours or PC-ACE), aggregating disaggregated data via SQL insert or update queries may require contextual knowledge to disambiguate the meaning of words that have different meanings depending on context (for instance, "throw" stones, which is an action of violence, and "throw" a proposal on the table, which is an action of bargaining). A proper aggregation of ambiguous words would require the costly process of going back to the original documents. To avoid this, you may want to consider a strategy where you code both the original wording and the aggregated code (but never just the aggregated code . . . unless you have no choice).[18]

5. The ambiguity of the meaning of words may also lead you to abandon one of content analysis's tenets: That only mutually exclusive categories should be used and that information should be coded only in one category may not work in practice. You may wish to use multiple aggregate codes, placing the same information into different aggregates.

summary_table

Let us summarize the main points encountered in this chapter in this summary_table:

ID	Point
1	No computer software, no quantitative narrative analysis. The application of complex story grammars beyond trivial examples requires a computer implementation.
2	Artificial Intelligence, in its approach to computer understanding of natural languages, is getting closer to having a fully automated approach to textual analysis, but it is not there yet. Nonetheless, some AI applications are available (e.g., KEDS, IDEA) that provide a minimal approach to quantitative narrative analysis. They allow you to automatically code the subject, the action, and the object (the minimally SAO part of a story grammar). Beware! This type of software (namely, KEDS, IDEA) currently only processes titles of news wires; furthermore, such software may lead to duplications of SAO structures (a dangerous outcome if you are involved in historical research; you don't want to end up multiplying real, historical events).
3	Commercially available CAQDAS software packages for qualitative data analysis (e.g., ATLAS.ti, N6, NVivo, MAXQDA, WinMax) work best for "thematic" content analysis but provide some capabilities for quantitative narrative analysis.
4	ETHNO and AutoMap are freeware software based on structures that are essentially story grammars. Their use for QNA, however, is very limited.
5	You could implement a minimal story grammar with only the SAO elements (subject, action, and object) even in a three-column rectangular spreadsheet. But a complex story grammar is fundamentally a relational structure that requires a relational database design for optimal representation (e.g., Oracle, Microsoft ACCESS, FoxPro).
6	PC-ACE (Program for Computer-Assisted Coding of Events, available for free download at www.pc-ace.com) is a relational database management system (RDBMS) application of Microsoft Access that I designed to carry out quantitative narrative analysis. PC-ACE has several features designed for optimal quantitative narrative analysis (e.g., setup of a specific story grammar,

(Continued)

(Continued)

ID	Point
	maximization of data-entry speed and data reliability, data query and data update). In contrast to all commercially available qualitative data analysis software packages (e.g., ATLAS.ti), PC-ACE does not expect the texts to be analyzed to be imported into the software. All information is entered manually by a user via text or combo boxes in specialized data entry forms taking it from an external document (a microfilm, a book, a digitized document).
7	In a relational database, a simple language (SQL, Structured Query Language) based on a handful of statements (*select, from, where, count*) allows you to extract data from the database in very general ways. SQL can be used not only to query the database but also to perform automatic updates and inserts of records (features that are extremely useful in the process of data cleaning and data aggregation).
8	The trick in going from words to numbers, or analyzing words statistically, is very simple: You count the words, and you apply statistical procedures on the numbers that result from those counts. Having objects in a relational database makes counting more meaningful in terms of quantitative narrative analysis. You don't count the frequency of unrelated objects but the frequency of selected objects (e.g., subjects) in relation to other objects (e.g., actions) and for specific values of each (e.g., the actions performed by the subject "fascists").
9	The organization of QNA coding should take into account how humans process information, stories, in particular. Be aware of the role of the reader!

Notes

1. In the rapidly expanding and volatile market of textual analysis software, where products come and go, printed reviews always lag behind (nonetheless, see Popping, 2000, appendix; Lewins & Silver, 2007; see also Alexa & Zuell, 2000). There are several Web sites on textual analysis and content analysis resources that *may* be more up-to-date. Yet even those quickly become stale as the curators of these pages give up on the task of keeping up with such a rapidly changing market.

103

I would recommend doing Web searches using key words such as "textual analysis" or "content analysis," and "software" or "computer programs," and "resources" or "help" to pull up available sites.

2. Scanners typically come with free optical recognition program software (you can also download them free from the Web), although commercial optical recognition software such as OmniPage Pro might be a better option. With good quality print you can usually scan a page and convert it in about 2 minutes. The problems arise with poor-quality print. Such pages can take quite a bit of time to check (and correct) for errors. Most optical recognition software packages have a pop-up box, somewhat like the more familiar spell check in MS Word, that opens every time it does not recognize a word. Typically, the best of these types of software learn from their mistakes and get better with time. Large files also really slow down the process (but they also slow down ATLAS.ti; thus, using several small files where possible is a good idea (there are no limits to how many documents can be assigned in ATLAS.ti).

3. See www.wjh.harvard.edu/~inquirer/, www.webuse.umd.edu:9090/, and www .wordscores.com (Laver, Benoit, & Garry, 2003; Stone, Dunphy, Smith, & Ogilvie, 1966).

4. For an evaluation of computer approaches to content analysis, see Franzosi (2008, pp. xxx–xxxii).

5. Older types of mainframe textual analysis software, such as Textpack and SPAD-T (like other types of text analysis software such as Wordsmith), provide useful frequency distributions of words or of words in context. SPAD-T will also perform statistical analyses of textual data in the French tradition of *analise des données textuelles* (Ludovic, Alain, & Mónica, 1989). No doubt, Textpack or SPAD-T can be very useful in allowing investigators to highlight fundamental characteristics of a text *qua text*. As Guerin-Pace (1998) writes, "The use of statistical methods of textual analysis [in the form of factor analysis and graphical representations] offers an extremely rich exploratory approach" (p. 73). But even less so than N6, MAXQDA, or ATLAS.ti are Textpack and SPAD-T suited for quantitative narrative analysis. They would provide useful analytical tools for mapping graphically clusters of words, for testing hypotehses about discourse, rather than action (see also the routines of HOMALS, http://cran.r-project.org/web/packages/homals).

6. ETHNO, designed by Heise (1989; Corsaro & Heise, 1990), and AutoMap, designed by Carley (1993, 1994; Diesner & Carley, 2004), are available for free download at http://www.indiana.edu/~socpsy/ESA and http://www.casos.cs.cmu .edu/projects/AutoMap.

7. AutoMap is preset on seven main classes of entities: agent, knowledge, resource, task-event, organization, location, and attribute. But, in contrast to ETHNO, the user can define as many new categories as his research requires or change the name of preset entities.

8. For an application of ETHNO, see Griffin's (1993) analysis of the narrative of a 1930 lynching in Mississippi.

9. Data for this project were stored in a spreadsheet (P. Oliver, personal communication, February 23, 2009).

10. For an easy introduction to SQL, see Dietrich (2001); for more challenging approaches, linked to database design, see the classics by Date (1987), Ramakrishnan and Gehrke (2002), and Elmasri and Navathe (2006).

11. It is not only cognitive psychologists who ask these questions of a story. Historians will ask those same questions of their documents. The historical "sciences," Rickert (1902/1962) wrote,

> Do *not* aim at the discovery of natural laws or even at the formation of *general* concepts . . . They do not *want* to produce "ready-made" clothes that fit Paul just as well as they do Peter; they propose to represent reality, which is never general, but always individual, in its *individuality*. (p. 55)

Sociologists (and the social sciences more generally) are less inclined to ask questions of stories, to deal with individual stories. Their goal is to generalize. Windelband (1894/1980) labeled the first kind of sciences "idiographic," and the second "nomothetic," dedicated to the discovery of general laws. Yet asking questions of a story that deal with the fundamental structural features of a story (who did what, when, where, and why)—particularly when these questions cut across thousands of stories—may be a good starting point for generalization.

12. PC-ACE achieves its flexibility through the following steps:

- You start with a simple object (simplex) that you can define as text, number, Boolean, or date.
- Each object can be set up as required or optional, as occurring once or many times.
- On that object, you can set up different validation rules to restrict and check what is entered in it (e.g., a date cannot be prior to January 1, 1919, or posterior to December 31, 1922).
- On that object, you can set up different functions to manipulate the information contained in the object: First, Last, MINimum, MAXimum, Average, Count . . .
- That object can be combined with one or more similarly defined objects to create complex objects (e.g., the complex object <name>, made up of the simplex text fields <first name> and <last name>).
- Within complex objects, you can set up different validation rules across simple objects to restrict and check the relationships of the information entered in different simplex (e.g., an actor coded as "employer" cannot "strike" but can "lockout").
- You can set up different types of relationships between objects: hierarchical (one-to-many relationship, such as a <dispute>, an <event>, or a <semantic triplet> in our narrative grammar) or relational (same level), defined as one-to-one.
- You can display any stand-alone simplex or simplex within complex as part of any other object.

- Simplex and complex can be arranged in specific sequences to provide meaningful ways of understanding the data (thus, in a <semantic triplet>, the <action> comes after the <subject>).
- For every object you can retrieve its history (i.e., who created or modified the object, and when).
- For every object you can retrieve its source (i.e., from which specific document the information was taken).
- This data structure, made up of simplex and complex objects, can be modified at any time during data collection, adding, modifying, deleting objects (or moving their position within the structure).
- Within and across simplex and complex, you can query the database for any kind of information in very general ways.
- Data stored in simplex and complex can be exported, in general ways via SQL queries, for use within more specialized data analysis software (from UCINET to SPSS, ARCGIS to STATA).

13. Figure 3.12 also shows an EQL button. EQL, Extended Query Language, was developed by Benedict Elliott-Smith for an easy interface between SQL, which requires knowledge of the table structure, and the user, who has knowledge only of the story grammar he/she set up. Although Fabio Cunial developed an even easier approach to querying the database via the GUI Query Manager, EQL can still be useful when the GUI runs out of stack space.

14. Certainly, if you design your own database system, you want to make sure to apply restrictions on the values that can be entered in certain fields or even across fields—a date of 1987 is very unlikely in a historical project on the period from 1919 to 1922 and so is the noun "employers" as the subject of a triplet "employers strike."

15. It would be a straightforward programming task to import the original text documents into the PC-ACE database. It has not been a priority for me since, in my work, I was using microfilms of historical documents as data sources. Importing tens of thousands of documents into the database would have made even more expensive an already expensive research project.

16. The software should provide a range of alternative printing formats of the coded information: Printing each item of coded information with all the coding labels, with all the information in basic narrative format but without labels, or even without the modifiers for quick access to the basic skeleton triplet structure of subject, action, and object. Different types of display allow coders to check for different types of breakdown in coherence. Printing output with the appropriate coding labels would enable a reader to catch text coded under the wrong category (for example, "gun" wrongly coded under the label <reason> rather than <instrument>).

17. The PC-ACE "Story view" form displays the output of a dispute, event, or single triplet in narrative form, along a basic SAO template. In its default format, the form displays both coding categories (in black) and coded information (in blue). It also displays (in gray) a succinct summary of the information coded (the identifier). Comments by both coders and verifiers can also be displayed (in red and

orange). The form allows the user to change print format, to zoom in on any of the objects displayed, to add verifiers' comments to any object that shows a breakdown of basic semantic coherence, and so on.

18. A good software package could be programmed to provide automatic suggestions for the choice of the aggregated code most appropriate for a specific disaggregated code, which would depend on the frequency distribution of the aggregated codes for a specific disaggregated code under consideration.

CHAPTER 4. THINGS TO DO WITH WORDS

Question and Answer (What Can You Do With Words?)

Question

What kind of things can you do with "thousands of words in the computer?" Or, as a social scientist would most typically put it, How can you analyze words?

Answer

There are a lot of things that you can do with words. If you want to stay in the realm of words, that is, analyze words qua words, as a linguist or a literary critic would do, then you have been reading the wrong book (although I hope to have given you a sufficiently long bibliography to take it from here). But I want to show in this chapter how to analyze words with quantitative tools, the last leg of this journey from words to numbers, from traditional forms of statistical analysis (namely, regression models) to forms of data analysis that have a one-to-one mapping with properties of narrative: network analysis, which takes advantage of the SAO structure of narrative, of the relations between social actors via their actions; event history and time-series analysis, based on the timing and duration of events; sequence analysis, to analyze the temporal order of skeleton narrative sentences (the story); and geographic information systems (GIS), based on knowledge of the time and space where given types of actions by given types of actors occur. I also explore the relationship between QNA and QCA, another mixed-method approach to social science questions. None of these techniques ever let us forget that "there are people behind numbers," as French historian Michelle Perrot put it (cited in Franzosi, 2004b, p. 241). For these analyses, I rely on PC-ACE and the data extracted from my *Il Lavoro* and *Avanti!* databases on the rise of Italian fascism.

Notice: statistical analyses are presented in this chapter as exemplars of the kinds of things to do with words, rather than full-fledged investigations into the rise of Italian fascism, leading to substantive, theoretical, and historical claims. The findings of the analyses, interesting and plausible as they are, are limited in several ways for me to make bold claims: (1) data cleaning and aggregation of the data are still under way; (2) for some analyses (e.g., QCA), the sample

108

of events analyzed represents a small subset of the events that led to the rise of Italian fascism; and (3) covariates are drawn almost exclusively from elements taken from *within* the stories themselves (e.g., event history analysis and QCA); after all, events occur in conjunction with other events, not necessarily included in a database of conflict narratives (e.g., the levels of unemployment or inflation rate, conditions known to affect the probability of conflict).

Traditional Statistical Analyses (Regression Models)

It is the organization of words in a relational database, with all relevant narrative elements (e.g., actor, action, time, space) organized in separate but interconnected files that makes it possible to get numbers out of words. In such a relational database, through SQL (Structured Query Language) and its handful of general commands (in particular, *select, from, where*) you can navigate a database in search of who did what, when, where, and why. The *count* statement within a *select* clause can provide the number of occurrences of entries in a given column. This way, by counting, words can be transformed into numbers; variables can be constructed; hypotheses can be tested.

Take the so-called red menace hypothesis in relation to the rise of Italian fascism (Brustein, 1991; for this example, see Franzosi, 2004b, pp. 115–118). The question is, was Italian fascism a reaction to socialism, a reaction to the menace of the red years of 1919 and 1920, the red guards standing armed on factory rooftops during the factory occupation movement? If that's the case, we would expect a close geographic overlap between working-class mobilization during the red years (1919–1920) and fascist countermobilization during the "black years" (1921–1922). In terms of a simple OLS model, we could specify this hypothesis in the following terms: the level of fascist violence in 1921 in a province depends on (1) the extent of social conflict from below in that province during the red years and (2) the percentage of towns in the province that obtained a socialist majority during the administrative elections of November 1920. The statistical model (red menace hypothesis) is

$$Y_i = \beta_0 + \beta_1 X_{1i} + \beta_2 X_{2i} + \varepsilon_i \qquad (4.1)$$

where

- the subscript i indexes the set of 57 provinces on which the regression is run ($0 < i < 58$);
- Y_i refers to the number of fascist violent actions in province i in 1921;
- X_{1i} refers to the number of working-class conflict events in province i during the red years of 1919 and 1920;
- X_{2i} refers to percentage of towns in province i that obtained a socialist majority during the administrative elections of November 1920; and

- the expected signs of the parameters are $\beta_1 > 0$ and $\beta_2 > 0$, with β_0 being a constant measuring the intercept.

If the red menace hypothesis were correct, we would expect a violent fascist reaction in those provinces where the middle and/or upper classes may have felt threatened by the level of working-class mobilization in their provinces.

To estimate this model, we need measures of Y_i, X_{1i}, and X_{2i}. Measures of X_{2i} of electoral returns can be taken from available political sources. Measures of Y_i can be taken directly from the *Avanti!* database via SQL queries that extract the number of conflict actions committed by workers and socialists and the number of violent actions committed by the fascists in each province.

The OLS-estimated model (red menace hypothesis) would then be

$$Y_i = 2.835^* + .125^* X_{1i} + .7176^* X_{2i}, \qquad (4.2)$$

where all the estimated coefficients are significant at the .01 level and the R^2 is .573. The regression evidence seems to support the red menace hypothesis: provinces with higher levels of working-class mobilization lead to significantly higher levels of fascist countermobilization.

Exploiting the Properties of Narrative

Starting from words, we have estimated a typical statistical OLS model based on quantitative variables. We have gone from words to numbers. And those numbers tell us something statistically significant and historically meaningful about the rise of Italian fascism. Unfortunately, in this type of statistical model, the social actors of the period as found in the original narratives (the police, the socialists, the workers, the fascists, the conflict, the violence) have disappeared, hidden behind variables. Time and space have also disappeared behind an index, *i*. Is there a way to quantify and generalize through numbers without losing sight of the fundamental properties of narrative (actors and their actions, time, duration, space, and temporal sequences)? We seek answers to each of these questions next.

Actors and Their Actions: Network Models

Narrative, at its core, is a story of action. And that action is what actors do. Narrative, in other words, tells us something about the relationship between social actors. In our SAO structure, both S and O are typically social actors tied together by the action, A. There is a class of statistical tools that is perfectly suited to dealing with relationships between actors, tools that mirror the SAO structure: network models. In network models, the S and O are known as "nodes" (rather than actors), and the actions between the nodes are known as "relations." Network models represent these relations graphically through directed graphs between nodes (basically, a line with an arrowhead, →). Thus, in a relation where fascists beat up socialists, the directed graph would go from fascists to socialists. And if workers burn landlords' barns, the graph would go from workers to landlords. If the frequency of violence varies between different social actors (nodes), the thickness of the various graphs could be varied to reflect these different frequencies. But using actors as network nodes is just one of several options available for network analysis with narrative-type data. Another option, pursued by Wada (2004), is using claims (or reasons for action) as nodes. Using this strategy with newspaper data, Wada effectively shows the increasing politicization of claim networks in Mexico between 1964 and 2000.

The estimate of network models requires the construction of square matrices (one square matrix for each sphere of action, e.g., violence, conflict, threat, communication, facilitation), where rows and columns represent different social actors and entries in each cell provide counts of actions from one row-actor toward another column-actor (e.g., 78 violent actions from fascists against socialists).[1] Each layered matrix would allow us to provide descriptive network graphs (Wasserman & Faust, 1994).

In practice, the creation of network matrices would involve extracting from the database via SQL the Subject, Action, and Object around a specific sphere of action (e.g., violence). Furthermore, if you wish to restrict these network graphs to given periods and places, you would also need to extract the time and location of each triplet. Then, for the selected period and place, you need to compute counts of violent actions between each pair of actors in the matrix. Let's do just that, using the PC-ACE Query Manager on the *Avanti!* database, for relations of violence (see Figure 4.1).

The query of Figure 4.1 will extract 5,215 records of violence, saved as a PC-ACE user table (see Figure 4.2).

The PC-ACE network analysis form (Figure 4.3) and the Visual Basic code behind it will then use the data in the saved user table to automatically compute the network matrix necessary to run network models.

The ASCII output matrix generated by PC-ACE can then be imported (or just copied and pasted) into a network analysis software (e.g., UCINET, Pajek) to compute network graphs (see Figure 4.4 for the data matrix copied and pasted into UCINET). The matrix data show that a number of social actors were involved in violence, as agents or targets.

On the basis of these data, and focusing on those nodes (actors) with the strongest ties (i.e., highest number of cases of violence), you can generate the network graph of Figure 4.5.[2]

The graph provides a stark representation of the actors involved in the violence (fascists and police) and the targets of their violence (communists, socialists, and workers but also ordinary citizens). The graph also shows evidence of violence between workers and landlords and industrial entrepreneurs. (For similar network graphs based on the *Il Lavoro* data, see

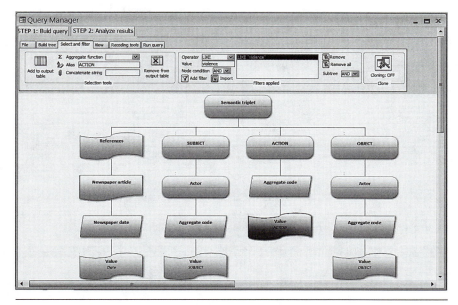

Figure 4.1   PC-ACE Query Manager: Querying for Network Data

Franzosi, 1999, and Franzosi, 2004b, pp. 100–108; for exploratory analyses of *Il Lavoro* data, see Franzosi, 1997.)

Of course, given what we know about those years, we may wonder whether the social relations of violence changed over time between the red years (1919–1920) and the black years (1921–1922). The network graphs of

DATE	SUBJECT	ACTION	OBJECT
1/10/1919	workers (agriculture)	violence	landlords
1/16/1919	workers	violence	workers
1/16/1919	workers	violence	workers
1/19/1919	police	violence	workers
2/26/1919	entrepreneurs	violence	politicians
5/9/1919	police	violence	socialists
5/10/1919	entrepreneurs	violence	workers
5/11/1919	workers	violence	workers
5/14/1919	police	violence	workers
5/14/1919	entrepreneurs	violence	workers

⊞ usertable:SAO

Record: I◄ ◄ 1 of 5215 ► ►I ►✳ 🍇 No Filter | Search

Figure 4.2   PC-ACE Query Manager: Query Results (Network Data)

112

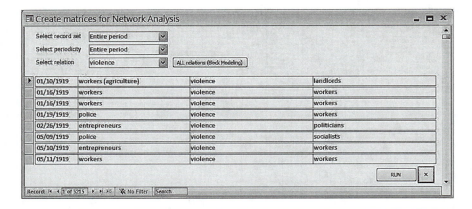

Figure 4.3   PC-ACE Form for the Creation of Network Matrices

	workers (agriculture)	landlords	workers	police	entrepr...	politicia...	socialists	citizens	fascists	professi...	shopke...	war affe...	commu...	magistry
workers (agriculture)	19	7		20		1	7	2	17					
landlords	32						2							
workers			36	53	16	3	4	1	110	5	1	1		
police	72		246	27	6	11	72	113	35	9	3	13	6	
entrepreneurs			41	1	1	1	3	9	2					
politicians	1		9	1		1	3	1	1	1			1	
socialists			3	14	1		6	1	85	1				
citizens			3	20	1	1			38					
fascists	179	1392	72	17	131	1006	445	81		70	34	41	166	7
professionals														
shopkeepers														
war affected			3	2					3			1		
communists			2	3			10	1	70	1				
magistry														

Figure 4.4   UCINET Data Matrix (Relations of Violence, 1919–1922)

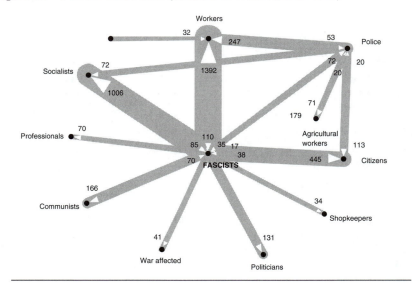

Figure 4.5   Network Graph for the Sphere of Action of Violence (1919–1922)

113

Figures 4.6 and 4.7, again focused on the stronger ties, clearly show that, indeed, the matrix of violence changed: During the red years, the graph is a typical "star" network, where the police occupy the center of the star and

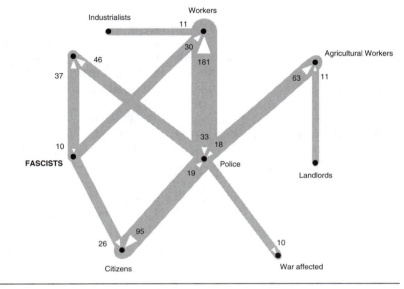

Figure 4.6   Network Graph for the Sphere of Action of Violence (1919–1920)

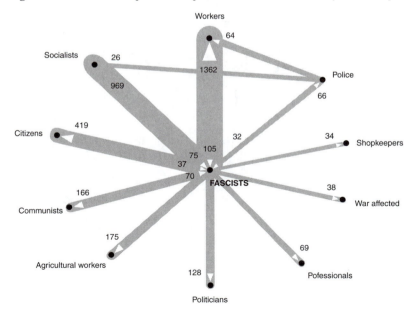

Figure 4.7   Network Graph for the Sphere of Action of Violence (1921–1922)

114

commit most of the violence in a climate of high working-class mobilization; during the black years, the center of violence has shifted from the police to the fascists and has increased manifold in frequency. The police are eerily absent.

Time (and Duration): Time-Series Models[3]

Genette's (1980) *Narrative Discourse: An Essay in Method* is a book in five chapters, three of which bear the titles "Order," "Duration," and "Frequency." The chapters deal with the fundamental temporal nature of narrative. Reflecting this feature of narrative, a great deal of the data delivered by QNA are time series in nature (i.e., data points indexed by time). Consider the time-series plots of Figure 4.8 of the number of workers' actions of conflict and fascists' violent actions between 1919 and 1922. The plots summarize in graphical form the combined query results reported in Figures 3.17 and 3.18. Even a quick glance at the plots reveals distinctive *temporal* patterns:

1. High levels of working-class conflict during the red years of 1919 and 1920 and decline during the black years, following the factory occupation movement of September 1920

2. Negligent levels of fascist violence during the red years and surge during the black years of 1921 and 1922, starting *right after* the decline in working-class mobilization

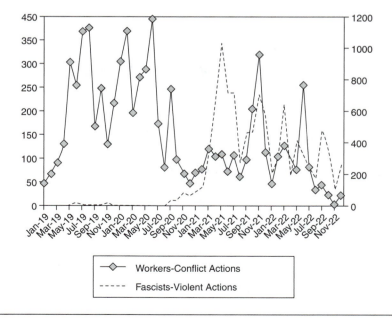

Figure 4.8   Workers' Mobilization and Fascists' Countermobilization

3. A jagged, up-and-down behavior of the plots, with peaks and troughs

4. An apparent "hand in hand" occurrence of the up-and-down cycles of the two plots of workers' conflict and fascists' violence for the black years

These ups and downs in the plots of Figure 4.8 reveal a *cyclical* behavior in working-class mobilization and fascist countermobilization that is altogether typical of time-series data. Yet the plot of Figure 3.9 of the number of strikers between 1879 and 1921 revealed another characteristic of time-series data: the *trend*. A trend refers to the long-term behavior (up, down, stationary) of time series (and what is a trend may be a cycle in a long-term perspective).

What explains the short- and long-term dynamic of time-series data? What explains trends and cycles? Furthermore, are cycles periodic or non-periodic (i.e., do cycles peak at fixed intervals and after fixed time lengths, e.g., every 4 months, every 6 months, or every few years)? What is the like-lihood of an event of fascist violence to occur at any given time and/or to have a given duration? These are the questions that a number of statistical models dealing with time-dependent data attempt to answer, from tradi-tional econometric models to spectral analysis, ARIMA models, and event history models.[4] Each approach focuses on different aspects of time and answers different questions about time.

My early work on strikes in post–World War II Italy (1950–1980) was based on official strike statistics (namely, number of strikes, strikers, and hours lost) and econometric and spectral techniques (Franzosi, 1995). Spec-tral analysis studies the distribution of the variance of a time series with fre-quency. It reveals the presence of periodic cycles in a time series (i.e., a cycle that repeats itself with predictable regularity: monthly, quarterly, yearly, every 3 years). The use of these data and methods allowed me to pin-point some basic facts about Italian strikes:

1. The negative relationship between strikes and unemployment as brought out by econometric models (Franzosi, 1995, pp. 30–55)

2. The strong, reciprocal relationship between trade unions' organiza-tional capacity and strikes (Franzosi, 1995, pp. 96–142)

3. The cyclical and period nature of Italian strikes, with a 3-year cycle in strike indicators due to the renewal of national, industrywide con-tracts of 3 years' duration, brought out by spectral analysis and con-firmed by econometric models (Franzosi, 1995, pp. 143–189)

4. The "out-of-phase" relationship between number of strikes and number of strikers (i.e., a 1-year lag between peaks in the two series) revealed by spectral techniques and due to the structure of collective bargaining in Italy in the 1970s and 1980s (with industrywide, national contract renewals every 3 years, reflected in a spike in the number of

strikers, followed by local, firm-level contract renewals and reflected in a spike in the number of strikes) (Franzosi, 1995, pp. 143–189)

QNA delivers information that can be easily turned into time-series data in the form of event counts (as in Figure 4.8). For this type of data, econometrics, spectral, and ARIMA models no doubt provide ideal tools of analysis. When it comes to QNA data, however, event history analysis may offer an even more ideal tool of analysis (on the use of this technique for narrative data, see Elliott, 2005, pp. 77–88). In event history analysis, we find the language familiar to QNA of event, time, and duration. But we also find a new and useful concept: risk (also known as propensity or probability), the risk that an event will occur at any given time, perhaps in relation to other covariates. Event history analysis is particularly well-suited to studying issues such as the duration of events, the temporal interval between events of a specific type (e.g., strike, demonstration, fascist violence), or the interval between certain types of event and other types of event (e.g., a trade union reaction to a government action, or a fascist attack as a response to a socialist protest). In all these cases, event history analysis estimates the risk of an occurrence.

To test the power of event history analysis in relation to QNA data, using SQL queries on the *Avanti!* database, I extracted a subset of 933 violent disputes during the period from 1921 to 1922. I pose three questions to these data:

1. Does the temporal interval between any two violent disputes narrow as the number of violent events in the immediately preceding days rises?

2. Do the types of main actors involved in disputes (namely, socialists or fascists) in the immediately preceding days have any effect on the length of the interval between disputes?

3. Is the rate of occurrence of violent events linked to the timing of specific historical events (e.g., political elections of May 15, 1921)?

To find an answer to these questions, I used the following covariates in a Cox regression model: (1) the number of disputes that started in the first available preceding dispute (to answer the first question); (2) the most frequent actor and the actor who started the dispute in the first available preceding dispute (to answer Question Number 2); and (3) the "historical setting" (Blossfeld & Rohwer, 1995, p. 10), measured here by a set of dummy variables, one for each of the 24 months of the black years, as a proxy for unmeasured political, social, and economic covariates (to find an answer to Question Number 3).

The Cox regression estimates are reported in Figure 4.9 as the odds ratios Exp(b) for both socialists and fascists plotted against time, where the odds ratios measure the risk or propensity of occurrence of a violent

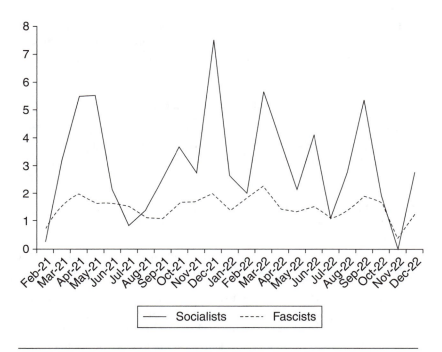

Figure 4.9   Exp(*b*) Parameters of Cox Model Relative to the "Historical Setting" Variable

dispute. For the socialists, all three hypotheses are supported. The greater the number of violent events in previous days, the shorter the interval between disputes, confirming the hypothesis that violent events can be the result of the prosecution of events started earlier. Even the main actors involved exert an influence. When the main actor is socialists or fascists, the interval between disputes shrinks by 70%. Finally, during the black years, unmeasured historical processes have a direct effect on the risk of violence and on the length of the interval between violent disputes. The plot shows that the distance between disputes varies with time. When the curve rises, the interval between disputes falls; when the curve falls, the interval between disputes rises.

The opposite is true for the fascists. The same covariates that explain the timing of socialists' actions do not work for the fascists. The effect of immediately preceding events is weak, and the effects of both the main actor and the timing of events disappear.

The findings help raise questions for further investigation. Is it possible that the fascists' violent acts were so temporally and spatially diffused and

118

systematic as to be rather insensitive to other events? Is it possible to think of fascists' violent events as not so much reactions to other events (perhaps violent) as violent acts whose only aim is (was) to create a diffused sense of terror, like the *Grande Peur* of 1789?

Paradox of a Journey (Two Recommendations)

Despite the robust statistical findings of my early work on Italian strikes, both data and methods had severe limitations, limitations that pushed me in this journey from words to numbers, "in search of the actor;" the role of social actors was lost, hidden behind econometric and spectral coefficients (Franzosi, 1995, pp. 15–18; 2004b, pp. 3–4). It may seem paradoxical that at the end of such a long journey, I should find myself back at my starting point, back at time-series models. Yet remember this:

1. The data that QNA has delivered are far richer than the "event counts" (namely, number of strikes) of my early strike research.

2. Time-series techniques are just one set of techniques that can be used with QNA data, just one answer to many research questions; after all, I set off in search of the actor, and no doubt, the actor I did find, as the findings from a variety of statistical approaches presented in this chapter confirm (*Recommendation 1:* don't put all your eggs in one basket).

3. Finally, if you want to find patterns in a large volume of quantitative data, nothing will serve you better than statistics (*Recommendation 2:* don't throw out the baby with the bathwater).

Temporal Order: Sequence Analysis[5]

It was Propp, the early-20th-century Russian formalist, who first claimed that the core actions of a story (what he called *functions* of a story) and their sequence form an invariant structure. Furthermore, the sequence in which those functions appear is fixed.[6]

Propp used a simple notation (ABC↑DEFG HJIK↓Pr . . .) to great effect to study the sequence of his 31 functions across his "working material consist[ing] of 100 tales" (Propp, 1928/1968, p. 24). Would modern methodology and computational power allow me to do better in the analysis of the sequences of thousands of events in my *Avanti!* database? To answer this question, I relied on Bison's (2009) approach to sequence analysis (on the use of sequence analysis for narrative data, see Elliott, 2005, pp. 88–90).

Sequence analysis is ideally suited to provide answers to questions such as the following: How does an event start, unfold, end? Were there typical patterns in the unfolding of violent events during the black years of 1921 and 1922? Do sequences of violence change in relation to the main social actors involved? Differently put, which roles do different actors play and in which order do they enter the fray? Did different patterns of violence occur at different times and places, or were they uniformly prevalent throughout the period? Do specific external events (e.g., the political elections of May 15, 1921) trigger specific types of sequences, reflecting specific strategies of violence?

Bison's approach is based on the following three steps: (1) compute a lexicographic index to define the distance/coordinates among sequences; (2) apply cluster analysis on the resulting indices to extract a small set of homogeneous groups; and (3) apply Markovian chains on the groups to be able to represent graphically the content of the cluster groups. The lexicographic index treats a single sequence as a point in an n-dimensional space. It is ideally suited to deal with "multiple parallel track sequences" (the three sequences of Subject, Action, and Object).

I applied these three steps to 9,409 triplets extracted from the *Avanti!* database and belonging to 933 stories (disputes) of violence during the period from 1921 to 1922. I first computed the lexicographic indices. I then applied a k-means cluster procedure to the 118 coordinates of the lexicographic index. Ten different cluster groups were identified, based on different combinations of subjects, actions, and objects (see Table 4.1). Each of the 10 groups represents a different sequential pattern of violence (in terms of the type and role of different actors). In Group 1, for instance, socialists and police play the main role, with the fascists as supporting actors. The actions are mostly actions of movement and control, followed by violence. The space, the city, is the place where the story unfolds. Group 6 displays one main actor—fascists—with a main action—violence—and a main object—socialists.

The application of Markov chains to the groups of Table 4.1[7] would allow us to compute the probability of transition between lemmas. The results can be displayed as a network graph that summarizes the structure of narrative, where each arc (directed line) represents the probability of a transition between lemmas and the arrow gives the direction of the sequential order.

Figure 4.10 displays the graphs for Group 1 of Table 4.1. A quick reading of the network graph shows that Group 1 has a complex narrative structure. Violence is in the background, with a great deal of movement around towns, where the police exercise actions of control over the socialists. Politicians and the magistracy also exercise authority over cities. Workers engage in actions of assembly and conflict in towns. In such

(Text continued on page 123)

Table 4.1 Group Composition by Main Subject, Action, and Object (Percent Values)

	Groups										
	1	2	3	4	5	6	7	8	9	10	Total
Subjects											
Socialist, communist	19.7	10.1	9.1	19.7	8.7	3.9	12.1	13.5	7.1	20.0	11.8
Fascists	41.2	49.1	62.1	49.2	51.4	87.0	53.8	43.1	53.4	43.4	53.7
Police	15.4	13.4	9.2	7.5	17.1	2.5	9.5	27.7	21.8	14.7	13.9
Workers	6.1	6.7	4.7	7.1	8.6	.9	7.6	4.4	6.1	.9	5.7
Actions											
Communication	9.1	6.8	5.7	8.3	7.2	2.6	6.2	5.6	4.3	3.8	6.0
Conflict	7.4	10.7	8.4	11.9	7.2	3.9	7.8	7.0	5.7	5.8	7.7
Control	10.4	8.3	7.2	7.1	9.5	5.1	8.4	17.4	11.9	13.0	9.8
Movement	22.6	20.4	18.8	17.0	13.7	13.6	18.9	20.5	17.1	15.1	17.8
Violence	25.3	32.7	41.9	35.2	37.8	65.5	36.9	28.9	38.1	29.6	37.5

		Groups										Total
Objects		1	2	3	4	5	6	7	8	9	10	
Socialist, communist		13.9	16.1	14.6	20.4	11.1	27.7	18.0	18.9	17.7	38.3	18.6
Fascists		8.7	10.2	8.5	5.4	14.3	3.4	6.0	11.7	6.9	27.0	9.5
Individual		4.8	3.9	6.4	4.6	3.5	5.1	6.0	3.5	5.1	5.3	4.8
Workers		2.9	5.5	5.6	5.3	11.1	7.2	6.3	6.1	7.3	2.8	6.4
Town		63.6	53.2	57.4	58.2	48.0	48.4	57.6	50.7	54.1	19.6	52.4
Total		*100.0*	*100.0*	*100.0*	*100.0*	*100.0*	*100.0*	*100.0*	*100.0*	*100.0*	*100.0*	*100.0*
Number of triplets		624	820	982	857	1,177	797	1,657	1,060	905	530	9,409
Number of events		49	57	87	98	93	132	160	92	83	82	933

122

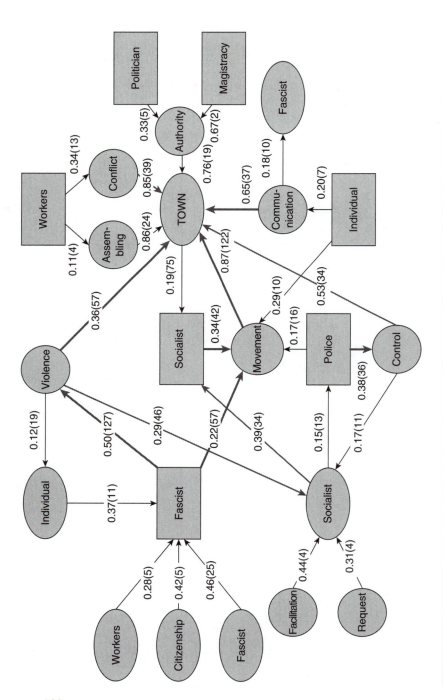

Figure 4.10 Network Graph of the Narrative Sequences of Group 1

123

(Text continued from page 119)
charged settings, fascists clash with socialists during workers' protests. Violence is directed against both things and individuals.

In contrast to this complex narrative structure, the narrative of Group 6 (graph not reported) is totally different—raw and essential. It captures the quick raid, the punitive expedition, where the fascists arrive, beat up, destroy, kill, and flee—the type of violence we encountered in the *Avanti!* article on the Lucca raid.

Sequence analysis is not meant as a confirmatory statistical tool. Rather, it serves an exploratory purpose. It points to patterns that require explanations. It generates research questions. Thus, Figure 4.11 reports the frequency distribution of violent actions for groups 1 and 6 during the black years. The plots seem to point to different strategies of violence adopted by the fascists. Group 6—the raid, the punitive expedition—seems to precede the May 15, 1921, political elections. As the election day approaches, violence moves to the city, in complex interactions with workers and socialists, during electoral rallies and strikes. The police exercises its control more on the victims than on the villains. These two strategies, although not so dramatically as around the national election of 1921, seem to go hand in hand during the entire period, as two alternative forms of violence (when one is up, the other is down, and vice versa). One more time, the strategies of different social actors come to the fore.

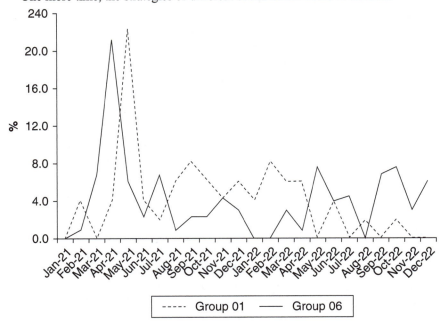

Figure 4.11   Frequency Distribution of Groups 1 and 2 During the Black Years (1921–1922)

124

Of Space (and Time): GIS

It is perhaps unfortunate that, in narrative theory, space occupies a less central role than time, with time, not space, as the sine qua non condition of narrative (after all, see Labov's, 1972, definition of narrative as "a series of *temporally* [emphasis added] ordered clauses" (pp. 360–361). Yet narrative theorists are hardly alone in their subordination of space to time. In her apology, *For Space,* Massey (2005) writes: "It seems in general to be perceived that space is somehow a lesser dimension than time . . . But life is spatial as well as temporal" (p. 29). Indeed, social actors move in time *and* space.

Swedish geographer Torsten Hägerstrand (1967) was among the first to point out that link, in his seminal work on the diffusion (in time and space) of innovative agricultural practices. Hedström (1994), building on Hägerstrand's work, showed how social structures affected the social diffusion of Swedish trade unions between 1890 and 1940, how "spatial properties and network densities are likely to influence considerably both the speed of a mobilization process and the success of a movement in organizing the relevant population" (p. 1176). In a seminal work of historical geography, English geographer Andrew Charlesworth (1979) showed how the Swing rebellion of 1830 in England moved south, day after day, along the river Thames, the main route of communication of the time. In one of modern history's classics, *The Great Fear of 1789,* Lefebvre (1956/1973) follows the spread of panic through rural France in 1789, day after day, village after village. At the heart of Lefebvre's, Charlesworth's, and Hedström's analyses is an attention to time, space, and, in Hedström's case, social structure.

GIS tools would be ideally suited to dealing with information such as time, space, actors, and actions (for an easy introduction to GIS, see Steinberg & Steinberg, 2006). Since this information is readily available in a relational database constructed on the basis of a story grammar, all we need is a set of SQL queries to extract the necessary data to be used in GIS software. We need a simple query to export the location (town) for the actions performed by different types of actors (e.g., workers, fascists). Town names can then be matched with geographic information of digitized maps of Italy, and, with the help of GIS software (e.g., ARCGIS or GRASS), maps can be produced to show diffusion processes or geographic overlaps between left-wing and right-wing actions/events.

It is on the basis of such data that I constructed the "hot points" map of the actions of conflict and of violence during the period from 1919 to 1922 (Figure 4.12). In hot points maps, areas of progressively greater incidence of conflict and violence are marked by different hues (e.g., from a light grey of less intensive areas to the black of more intensive areas). Milan and the region around it (Lombardy) are such hot points. The map also shows other hot areas, from Liguria (Genoa) and Piedmont (Turin) to Emilia Romagna

125

(the region of Bologna and Ferrara), Tuscany (where Florence is), Lazio (Rome), Campania (Naples), and Puglia. These hot areas broadly correspond to the areas that historians of the rise of Italian fascism have singled out—at least, if we go by the titles of the local histories they have produced (e.g., Bell, 1986; Colarizi, 1977; Corner, 1975; Snowden, 1986, 1989). But historians have not produced detailed maps of the conflicts of the period. The map of Figure 4.12 also has theoretical import for social scientists. The hot points on the map do seem to provide support to the red menace hypothesis that we visited in the early pages of this chapter. And yet the map of Figure 4.13 shows that the fascists' use of violence was much more pervasive, much more diffusive, than the red menace hypothesis warrants. Their attacks were systematic throughout Italy. Indeed, a count of the distinct locations in which workers and fascists were active would reveal a much higher number for the fascists. Many questions still remain to be answered about the rise of Italian fascism.

So there is much to be learned from space (especially from space *and* time together). *Historical time and historical space are one and the same.* To close with Massey (2005), "If time unfolds as change then space unfolds as interaction.

Figure 4.12 Hot Points Map of Actions of Workers' Conflict (1919–1920) and Fascists' Violence (1921–1922)

126

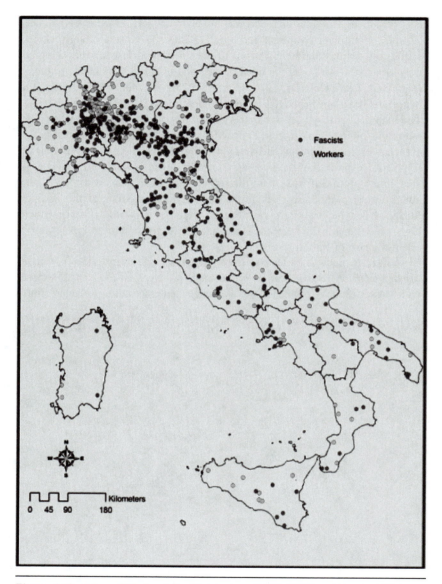

Figure 4.13   Map of Workers' Conflict Actions (1919–1920) and Fascists' Violent
Actions (1921–1922)

In that sense space is the social dimension" (p. 61). That calls forth the view
of "a relational politics for a relational space." The maps of Figures 4.12
and 4.13, however exploratory, speak of a spatially and temporally
constructed life as relational life. They speak of different social relations at

different times and in different places, of the conflict strategies of mobilizing and countermobilizing groups. Network and GIS interact here to provide a temporal and spatial map of the social relations of the rise of Italian fascism (or of lynching or of any other social phenomenon narratively represented).

The combined results of the statistical analyses may not allow us, as yet, to say a definitive word on the rise of Italian fascism, based on which interpretation holds best among the several categories shown in Table 4.1. But they leave no doubt about the role of social actors, the strategic choice of different courses of action, during those crucial years.

Linking Quality and Quantity: Where QNA and QCA Meet

Quantitative narrative analysis rests on the seminal work of Vladimir Propp (1928/1968). And that work was fundamentally comparative. "Let us compare the following events" (p. 19) he writes, with an eye to the question, "What do they have in common?"

> We are undertaking a comparison of the themes of . . . tales. For the sake of comparison we shall separate the component parts of fairy tales by special methods; and then we shall make a comparison of tales according to their components. (p. 19)

Through the comparison of hundreds of folktales, Propp highlights the invariant structures of these tales and their constitutive components and uses these components for further, systematic comparisons of the tales. Only comparison affords new knowledge. "If we are incapable of breaking the tale into its components, we will not be able to make a correct comparison. And if we do not know how to compare, how can we throw light upon . . ." (Propp, 1928/1968, p. 15).

Propp used the comparative method to find (and then test) an invariant structure of Russian folktales. I used Propp's structures to compare thousands of narratives of conflict and violence on the rise of Italian fascism. I make the claim that the QNA method provides a way to link quality and quantity. Another method, also fundamentally premised on comparison, makes a similar claim: Charles Ragin's QCA (Qualitative Comparative Analysis) approach (Ragin, 1987).

As Ragin and Rubinson (2009) write, "the *comparative method*— sometimes referred to as 'small-N comparison'—constitutes a distinctive approach to understanding social phenomena. Frequently, comparative methods are portrayed as a 'bridge' between qualitative, case-oriented research and quantitative, variable-oriented research" (p. 13). Furthermore, QCA is "fundamentally *set theoretic* in nature" (Ragin & Rubinson, 2009,

128

p. 13; see also Ragin, 1987, p. x). The same mathematical set theoretic "thin thread" thus underlies both QCA and QNA. And like QCA, where "each case is examined as whole" (Ragin, 1987, p. 49, see also pp. 16, 17, 56, 83, 166), QNA deals with "whole" event narratives, however incomplete these narratives may be. Both QCA and QNA, in other words, are holistic in their research strategies. Finally, although QCA and QNA fundamentally deal with qualitative data, both can cope with any number of cases or event narratives. In both approaches, there is a cost in large numbers, however. According to Ragin (1987),

> The case-oriented approach works well when the number of relevant cases is relatively small . . . As the number of cases and the number of relevant causal conditions increase . . . it becomes more and more difficult to use a case-oriented approach. (p. 49)

Or again, "The volume of comparison explodes as the number of . . . cases is expanded. The method simply becomes unwieldy" (Ragin, 1987, p. 68, see also p. 168). In QNA, comparisons can be carried out on thousands (rather than tens) of cases (i.e., event narratives, with each event narrative providing a case); but the cost of data coding is probably as high as the cost of coding in QCA all the relevant conditions for a large number of cases.

Question and Answer (How Do You Go From QNA to QCA?)[8]

Question

In QNA, events consist of sets of "semantic triplets." In QCA, events are listed, seriatim, in a "truth table," where, for each event under consideration, a handful of conditions deemed relevant for the occurrence of the event are set as present or nonpresent (Boolean values 1 and 0). How do you go from one to the other, from QNA to QCA?

Answer

Not different from network analysis or GIS, you start from an SQL query to extract from your database a set of conditions on a specific set of events. For the sake of illustration, suppose that we are interested in the conditions that led to fascist violence in 1921, extreme forms of violence in particular (killings, rather than breakings or nondeadly assaults). Our SQL query would search for all the events where the subject of at least one of the triplets in the event is "fascists," their actions are deadly (e.g., "kill"), and the year of occurrence is "1921" (basically, we set three restrictions via where clauses). Since QCA requires both positive and negative cases (i.e., fascist deadly and nondeadly events), we run a similar SQL query to extract the set of nondeadly events. When applied to my *Avanti!* database, the output of these SQL queries will be a few hundred events. Again, for the sake of illustration, let's randomly sample a more manageable set of events, and for these events let's extract a handful of conditions from the database itself: whether each killing occurred in the context of workers' collective actions (e.g., a strike or a rally), in an urban or rural setting, in the proximity of the political elections of May 15, 1921, and whether the police facilitated the fascists' actions (see the Excel spreadsheet of Figure 4.14).

1	Identifier	Workers' conflict	Elections	Urban	Police facilitation	Killings
2	Castellamare di Stabia 22.01.1921	1	0	0	1	1
3	Vigarano Mainada 26.02.1921	0	0	0	0	1
4	Casale Monferrato 08.03.1921	1	1	1	1	1
5	Cerignola 27.03.1921	1	0	0	1	1
6	Carmignano 30.03.1921	1	1	0	1	1
7	Persiceto 01.04.1921	0	0	1	0	1
:						
58	Ascoli Piceno 11.05.1921	1	1	1	1	0
59	Empoli 22.05.1921	0	1	1	0	0
60	Aquila 28.05.1921	0	1	1	0	0
61	Sala Bolognese 30.06.1921	0	0	0	0	0
62	Torino 23.06.1921	1	0	1	0	0
63	San Giorgio di Piano 29.06.1921	0	0	0	1	0
64						

Figure 4.14   Excel Input Data to QCA Based on a Sample of Fascists' Actions (1921)

The data in the Excel spreadsheet are then imported into Ragin's QCA software to create a truth table (QCA is available for free download at www.fsQCA.com). The results, reported in Table 4.2, show a truth table consisting of 16 rows, each row representing a different combination of the four independent variables ("causal conditions," in QCA terminology).

The truth table of Table 4.2 has classified the 62 cases from the original data set into 16 "types" of cases that resulted in fascist violence. The N column of Table 4.2 indicates how many cases conform to each causal configuration. Seven of these types of cases (Rows 2, 3, 7, 8, 9, 11, and 12) always resulted in killings. The nine other cases sometimes resulted in killings and sometimes not. Since QCA requires that a truth table be free of "contradictions," I used the rule: A causal configuration is said to "almost always result in fascist killings" if the corresponding cases resulted in killings at least 80% of the time (as reported in the "Killings %" column). As a result, the Killings column should be read as follows: This causal configuration did/did not almost always result in fascist killings. From the complete truth table (i.e., free of contradictions), QCA computes a set of Boolean solutions, that

130

Table 4.2   QCA Truth Table for a Sample of Fascists' Violent Actions
(1921)

Row	Conflict	Elections	Urban	Police	Killings	Killings (%)	N
1	1	1	1	1	1	80	5
2	1	1	1	0	1	100	4
3	1	1	0	1	1	100	1
4	1	1	0	0	0	50	2
5	1	0	1	1	0	50	2
6	1	0	1	0	0	42.9	7
7	1	0	0	1	1	100	7
8	1	0	0	0	1	100	3
9	0	1	1	1	1	100	2
10	0	1	1	0	0	33.3	3
11	0	1	0	1	1	100	3
12	0	1	0	0	1	100	3
13	0	0	1	1	0	33.3	6
14	0	0	1	0	0	60	5
15	0	0	0	1	1	80	5
16	0	0	0	0	0	50	4

is, it "reduces" the 16 lines of the truth table to a smaller set of Boolean equations, each equation representing one path to the outcome (i.e., fascist killings). In our case, QCA identifies five solutions (Table 4.3).

In the Boolean solutions equations, uppercase and lowercase values represent conditions that are, respectively, present and not present, + is read as the Boolean OR, and * as AND. These five solutions could be further reduced through a process of "factoring," by combining solutions with common terms (where this makes substantive sense). Equations 1 to 5 of Table 4.3, with several terms in common, may be factored in various ways. One option is as follows (Table 4.4).

Table 4.3   QCA "Boolean Solutions" for a Sample of Fascists' Violent Actions (1921)

1   ELECTIONS * POLICE +
2   urban * POLICE +
3   CONFLICT * ELECTIONS * URBAN +
4   CONFLICT * elections * urban +
5   conflict * ELECTIONS * urban

Table 4.4   QCA-Factored "Boolean Solutions" for a Sample of Fascists' Violent Actions (1921)

1a   POLICE (ELECTIONS + urban) +
2a   URBAN (CONFLICT * ELECTIONS) +
3a   urban ((CONFLICT * elections) + (conflict * ELECTIONS))

In Table 4.4, Equations 1 and 2 of Table 4.3 have been combined to form Equation 1a, which indicates that police intervention would almost always result in killings when that intervention occurred either (a) during an election period or (b) in a rural area. Equation 2a is simply a different way of expressing Equation 3 of Table 4.3 to highlight the contextual importance of location. It indicates that, in urban areas, killings almost always occurred during a workers' conflict during an election period. In rural areas, however, this combination frequently did not result in killings, as Equation 3a (which combines Equations 4 and 5 of Table 4.3) makes clear. Equation 3a reveals that, in rural areas, a workers' conflict usually resulted in killings only during nonelection periods. During election periods, it was the absence of a workers' conflict that resulted in killings.

Limited as these findings are, being based on a very small subsample of all violent events and on a very limited set of conditions, all internal to the narratives themselves, they do point to the advantages of combining mixed-method approaches (i.e., approaches that blur the line between quality and quantity, that use qualitative characteristics to build quantitative representations, whether in the form of Boolean mathematics or regular mathematics). Neither QNA nor QCA *hides the role of social actors behind statistical coefficients.* Furthermore, the various ways of factoring QCA solutions represent different ways of telling the same story. Thus, as with a story and plot, QCA provides the tools for exploring different ways to tell a story.

The "Thin Thread": Set Theoretic Mathematics

Regression models, and network, GIS, sequence, and event history models all give us different routes to the numbers in the journey "from words to numbers." Yet network models have a special appeal. The three basic tools involved in going "from words to numbers," or—in QNA–story grammars, relational database models, and network models are all based on the same underlying mathematics: set theory (Franzosi, 1994a, 2004b, pp. 89–91, 113–118). A thin mathematical thread links words to numbers, quality to quantity.

Linking the Micro and the Macro: Levels of Analysis

The hierarchical structure of a story grammar with different levels of data aggregation (macro event/dispute, event, semantic triplet) allows you to query the database at different levels and to extract (and then work with) different types of numbers. You can choose to work with the frequency distribution of individual verbs (e.g., "shout," or, at least, individual verbs aggregated into broader spheres, e.g., "violence") or with the frequency distribution of the events or macro events/disputes in which these verbs occur, with an individual actor (complete with name and last name) or institutions (e.g., the police, the Socialist Party). Similarly, you can choose to work at the street level, as much as at the neighborhood, city, province, or state level; or at the level of time of day, day, week, month, year, or the entire sample period of your project. The hierachical and highly disaggregated nature of QNA data will allow you to set your preferred level of analysis.

One More (Serious) Limit of QNA: Meaning of Action for the Actor

By allowing you to work at different levels of analysis, QNA provides one avenue for linking the micro and the macro, at least empirically. Theoretically, however, the problem of the micro-macro link remains. If Weber (1922/1978) is correct in claiming that "sociology . . . is a science concerning itself with the interpretative understanding of social action" (p. 4) and that "subjective understanding is the specific characteristic of sociological knowledge" (p. 15), the "realist" representation of sociohistorical reality that QNA provides, with its focus on observable actors and their actions, remains at the surface of that reality.[9]

The detailed knowledge of who does what, when, and where does not get us any closer to an "interpretative understanding of social action," to understand the deep-seated motivations that trigger social actors to act in specific ways. The qualitative social scientists discussed earlier (Chapter 2), who deal with words as words without turning them into numbers, may fare better after all. Reliance on "realist" newspaper accounts and story grammars to study the rise of Italian fascism or lynching would have to be combined with other sources (e.g., letters, diaries, and autobiographies) and other instruments of measurements (e.g., content analysis, if you want to quantify, or discourse analysis, if you want to stay in the realm of words). And, of course, your story grammar would have to be modified to include categories apt to capture meaning in the eyes of the actor.

Question and Answer (Which Substantive Applications?)

Question
Can you apply quantitative narrative analysis only to texts that describe violent events? Your examples seem to focus on violence and protest. Are there any other substantive applications?

Answer
Texts describing violent (or protest) events are prototypical narrative texts. Not surprisingly (and for good reasons), they end up being studied via coding schemes that have the basic characteristics of a story grammar (e.g., in Protest Event Analysis). But narrative also deals with a variety of human events other than protest and violence (e.g., Konstancya Walerych's move from Poland to the United States). For as long as the texts of interest—dealing with whatever type of events—are in narrative form, QNA can be applied.

Doyle (2009), for example, uses a simplified story grammar, based on actors, with their traits (physical and psychological) and their activities (classified as interactions, home, leisure, sport, play, school, work, beautification, and emotions),[10] to study gender, race, and ethnic representations in best-selling children's books in the United Kingdom (1964–2004). She analyzes a sample of 46 books and of 2,132 pages within these books from three different time points (1964, 1984, and 2004). Doyle's results, based on exploratory statistical work and network models, show that, over the three time points, the activities of work, home, emotions, play, and sport decrease, whereas those of leisure, school, and beautification increase. Interactions are the most frequent category of activities in all three time points and increasingly so over time.

White males are the most prominent group in all spheres of activity and interactions in 1964, apart from beautification, which is dominated by females. Nonetheless, females are not invisible: They are underrepresented, but they do engage in some activities, and there is even one female protagonist. This trend continues in 1984, but all groups are now more connected. Females appear as characters and protagonists more than they did in 1964; but the number of activities they engage in remains the same. The year 2004 is different from the previous time points. In this year, white females have become the most prominent category in all spheres of activity apart from work, which remains the domain of males, and all groups are more connected at this time point than in previous years. Females are underrepresented in terms of characters but overrepresented in the protagonist role. Differences in male and female activities are minimal. Yet even though home activities almost vanish in 2004, there are still more females performing this activity.

The portrayal of nonwhites shows less improvement over time compared with that of females. In both 1964 and 1984, nonwhites do act, in activities similar to those of the white characters, but they are depicted in terms of their relationship with the dominant group, rather than as a group in their own right. In 1984, nonwhites interact with whites—in fact, *only* with whites, rather than with members of their own group. School and sports are the only activities where nonwhites act more often than do whites. In 2004, the representation of the population at large is more accurate than before, with Asians being accurately depicted as the largest ethnic minority. Nonwhites are still mainly shown in the public domain, at work or at school, but on the occasions where nonwhites are shown engaging in home activities, they are being depicted as a group and are not just "token blacks."

Systems of Signs (Make All Implicit Information Explicit for the Computer)

What makes sense to you when you read a story that is syntactically and semantically correct within the rules of the natural language it is written in may turn out to be a problem when a computer has to make sense of that same story. To understand the problem, let's look at the gruesome narrative of a lynching event, a sad chapter of American history—one of many such events as I am currently coding for a project on lynching in Jim Crow U.S. South. The story appeared in a newspaper article published on July 16, 1921, by the *Washington Eagle* (reproduced in Ginzburg, 1962, pp. 152–153).

From Moultrie, Georgia, scene of the burning of the Negro Williams, the Eagle has obtained the following facts by an eyewitness . . . Williams was brought to Moultrie (Georgia) . . . five hundred poor pecks rushed on the armed sheriffs, who made no resistance whatever. They tore the Negro's clothing off . . . The Negro was unsexed and made to eat a portion of his anatomy which had been cut away. Another portion was sent by parcel post to Governor Dorsey, whom the people of this section hate bitterly . . . The Negro was taken to a grove, where each one of more than five hundred people, in Ku Klux ceremonial, had placed a pine knot around a stump, making a pyramid to the height of ten feet. The Negro was chained to the stump . . . The pyre was lit and a hundred men and women, old and young, grandmothers among them, joined hands and danced around while the Negro burned. A big dance was held in a barn nearby that evening in celebration of the burning, many people coming by automobile from nearby cities to the gala event. (Moultrie, GA, July 16, 1921)

The story makes sense to any "competent user of the (English) language." That competent user of the language would have no problem answering the following questions (some being "trick" questions): Did the sheriffs resist the assault of the crowd? Who tore off the Negro's clothing? Who took the Negro to a grove? Was the grove located in Atlanta, Georgia? Was the Negro chained to the stump on July 16, 1921? Was "the gala event" held in Savannah, Georgia, in the morning of August 19, 1931?

But a computer? Would a computer be able to answer those same questions? Computer scientists are getting closer in cracking the problem of computer understanding of natural languages. That is particularly true for language constructs made up of simple clauses and narrative sentences as in the story of Williams's lynching. But while we wait for computer scientists to put content analysts out of their misery by providing them with automatic sentence parsing, content analysts have to do the coding the hard way, through manual sentence coding; relevant information in the Williams story has to be entered manually by a human coder in the objects of a story grammar, stored in specific tables. In that computer system of signs, the way we would pose our initial questions would be through an SQL query of the type *"select* object *from* table *(where* condition)." To answer those questions, in other words, SQL would query a database looking for specific information in specific tables perhaps subject to specific conditions. In a computer system of signs, the story would have to be "rewritten" in slightly different form so that the computer has access to specific information as found in specific tables to answer specific questions.

Time and Space

Take time and space, the fundamental categories of narrative. Each narrative sentence in a story (i.e., a sentence where someone does something) is located in time and space. Typically, these temporal and spatial markers are given only once in a story. We are told that Williams's lynching occurred in Moultrie, Georgia, only once at the beginning of the story. Similarly, the date of the event is implicitly given by the date of the article. We can assume that all actions narrated in the story happened on that same day since no other date is introduced in the narrative. We are not told the time of the actions within the main lynching event: Early morning? Noon? Afternoon? We do not know. We can assume that they occurred during daytime only because the journalist writes, "A big dance was held in a barn nearby *that evening.*" There would

136

be no reason to mark the time of the "gala" ("evening") unless it happened at a different time from the other actions.

Although time and space are not repeated for every action in the story, a competent reader knows to impute time and space for every sentence, carrying them over from where these are given. Indeed, explicit temporal and spatial markers for every verb in a sentence would make the story nearly unreadable in the original system of sign of language itself. Imagine this:

> Five hundred poor pecks rushed on the armed sheriffs in Moultrie, GA, on July 16, 1921, who made no resistance whatever in Moultrie, GA, on July 16, 1921. They tore the Negro's clothing off in Moultrie, GA, on July 16, 1921. The Negro was unsexed in Moultrie, GA, on July 16, 1921, and made to eat a portion of his anatomy in Moultrie, GA, on July 16, 1921, which had been cut away, in Moultrie, GA, on July 16, 1921.

Would you continue reading a story that started this way? Yet that is exactly how the story would have to be written for computer understanding. The only way a computer would know when and where an action occurred (at least through an SQL query) is if you tell it explicitly, if you code time and space for every action or for every semantic triplet. Any query that extracted the time and space of action (e.g., because you need to use GIS tools) would leave out all actions with no time and space explicitly attached to them. Not surprisingly, the ATLAS.ti queries of what the fascists did in Lucca extracted only three records (see Figures 3.3, 3.4, 3.5, and 3.6), of the three triplets where Lucca was coded in the example of both PC-ACE and ATLAS.ti coding. To get a complete listing of all the actions carried out by the fascists in Lucca, you would need to code Lucca for every triplet.

The Participants in the Clause

For Halliday, participants in the clause are typically expressed as subjects and objects (as complements). In narrative, the participants—especially the subjects—are typically social actors (individuals, organizations, or, in fairy tales, anthropomorphic creatures). Again, the two systems of signs—natural language and SQL queries—require different forms of organization of the text for understanding. Take the clause "five hundred poor pecks rushed on the armed sheriffs, *who* made no resistance whatever." The clause contains two different sentences (or, in the categories of a story grammar, two different semantic triplets):

S: five hundred poor pecks   A: rushed on   O: armed sheriffs

S: who   A: made no resistance

When you use an SQL query to pull up all subjects stored in the database, a subject coded as "who" would hardly tell you anything about social relations (who is "who"?). You would need to code the "who" as "sheriffs." The same is true for other syntactical forms of participants in a clause. Take the following clause in the Williams lynching story: "They tore the Negro's clothing off." "They" refers to the 500 poor pecks (although probably not all of them).[11] Coding "they" as an actor would be meaningless when extracted by an SQL query.[12] Passive sentences suffer from the same ambiguity: "The Negro was unsexed and made to eat a portion of his anatomy which had been cut away." There is a great deal of ambiguity in the clause. Who did the unsexing? Again, presumably, the "five hundred poor pecks" (or at least some of them). And the people who made Williams eat a portion of his anatomy—were they the same ones who had done the unsexing, a subset of them, or different people among the "five hundred poor pecks"? For the benefit of the computer, your original story starts looking something like this:

> Five hundred poor pecks rushed on the armed sheriffs in Moultrie, GA, on July 16, 1921. The armed sheriffs made no resistance whatever in Moultrie, GA, on July 16, 1921. The five hundred poor pecks tore the Negro's clothing off in Moultrie, GA, on July 16, 1921. The five hundred poor pecks unsexed the Negro in Moultrie, GA, on July 16, 1921. The five hundred poor pecks made the Negro eat a portion of his cut away anatomy in Moultrie, GA, on July 16, 1921.

Similar to the original, but not quite the same. The requirements of different systems of sign (natural language and computer environment and SQL queries) require appropriate translations of the signs.

Of course, we don't run SQL queries for the sheer curiosity of pulling up records from a database. As social scientists, we pull up those records to run statistical analyses on those records (e.g., GIS, network analysis). These statistical analyses constitute yet another system of signs. Whereas a GIS system of signs requires location (and time if available) for every action mapped, the system of signs of network analysis requires both the subject and object participants of a clause as social actors to map social relations as directed graphs. Yet the sentence "who made no resistance whatever" in Williams's lynching story not only has an ambiguous subject (at least for an SQL query), it has no object; yet the implicit object of the sentence is those "five hundred poor pecks" who had rushed on the sheriffs. An SQL query aimed at extracting all the subjects, actions, and objects in your database for the purpose of running network models would not pull up this particular semantic triplet since it has no object and would not be part of your networks. It is the transitivity/intransitivity of the verb in a sentence that determines whether the sentence contains an object/complement or not. The clause "Workers went on strike today at the Barry Works after management laid off 200 workers" makes perfect sense in the system of signs of the English language. It still makes sense within the categories of a story grammar:

S: Barry Works management   A: laid off   O: 300 workers

S: Barry Works workers   A: went on strike

It will create problems, however, when you try to run network models since all actions of conflict based on intransitive verbs (e.g., strike, rally, picket) will not have one of the two nodes (actors, in the case of QNA) required by a network graph. To avoid biasing network models, be sure to code explicitly any implicit object of actions based on transitive verbs.

It is not just intransitive verbs that lead to potential problems. If you are planning to use network models for data analysis, even sentences with transitive verbs can lead to problems when the complement is a physical object. Let's go back to the *Avanti!* article of April 1, 1921, that describes the fascist attack on the Labor Chamber and Socialist Youth Club in Lucca. Nowhere in the clauses that make up the event narrative do we find a human complement for the verbs. A competent language user understands that the implicit object of the fascist violence is the "socialists"; the adjectives ("Labor" and "Socialist") attached to the complement "building" give it away. But an SQL query would pick up "building," and this would end up in a network graph without much sociohistorical meaning. After all, the purpose of network analysis in historical research is to map social relations among social actors (individuals or institutions and organizations).

Solutions to These Problems
(Back to the Golden Rules of QNA Coding)

Question

Is there anything that can be done to overcome these problems? After all, it was your recommendation to use network models and GIS.

Answer

The answer, of course, is "yes" (or I may not have asked that question . . .), and it goes along the following lines: Think ahead and think like a computer, about what you/it will need for data analysis. For time and space, you have several different rules that you can adopt for coding time and space, rules that must be added to the list of golden rules of QNA coding given in Chapter 3:

Rule Number 11: Code time and space for every action within a triplet (if you allow multiple actions within triplets).

Rule Number 12: Do not code time and space at the level of action (verb), but code them at the triplet level (you can then impute them automatically to every action within a triplet via SQL insert and update queries).

Rule Number 13: Code time and space at the level of event (and, again, automatically impute them to every action for every triplet within an event).

Whichever rule you adopt, adopt one only and use it consistently, or your SQL queries will not be able to pull out all the available records or will not pull them up accurately. Computers do not deal well with inconsistent behavior.[13]

Rule Number 14: Code explicitly any implicit social actor that is the intended target of an action where the verb is intransitive (e.g., strike) or the verb is transitive but the complement is a physical object (e.g., in the *Avanti!* account of Lucca fascists, the complements are "Labor Chamber" and "Socialist Youth Club," but the intended target is the "socialists").

Coding explicitly implicit objects will not distort network models since you can use this object/complement to run the SQL query that creates the input matrix for network analysis. It may not be generally possible to impute automatically a human or institutional target from a physical object since it may require context to disambiguate meaning (although in the specific case of the Lucca attack, an *insert* SQL query could add the implicit target "socialists" through a *where* condition listing the physical objects "Labor Chamber" and "Socialist Youth Club"; had the fascists knocked down the door of the custodian's house, automatic imputation would not have been as easy).

Notice: you do not need to code repeated objects from scratch every time (e.g., "who" coded as "sheriffs" or the same time and space repeated for every action or triplet). PC-ACE, for instance, allows you to link every repeated object to an existing object. This will not only save time, but in the case of participants, for instance, it will avoid multiplying historical actors. But remember: This option of linking objects must be programmed beforehand.

Question and Answer (How Many Triplets Do I Need?)

Question
A total of 18,000 documents; 140,000 semantic triplets. This is a daunting task. I am a graduate student considering QNA for my research project. I don't have the luxury of the 25 years it took you to collect those data and of your grants and team of coders. Is there anything meaningful I can say with QNA on the much smaller data set I could afford to collect?

Answer

Definitely. You don't need to code 18,000 documents and analyze 140,000 triplets to be able to extract meaningful patterns from QNA data. After all, Doyle, for her doctoral work, coded 8,483 semantic triplets from 2,132 pages from a sample of 44 best-selling children's books, and Vicari, for her doctoral work, coded 5,462 clauses, yielding 5,462 semantic triplets, from a sample of 222 social fora. And their findings are quite meaningful!

Significant Points

When it comes to the statistical analysis of words, several significant points we have touched on are worth highlighting:

1. Through counting, words can be analyzed statistically.

2. In traditional content analysis, the numbers made available by counting words have been analyzed with factor analysis and regression analysis.

3. Although these statistical techniques can still be applied to data made available by quantitative narrative analysis, other statistical techniques that have a more homologous relationship with narrative data can also be applied, techniques that fundamentally mirror the properties of narrative: network models, event history analysis, sequence analysis, and GIS.

   (a) Network models (and their graphical representations of relations among social actors around a specific sphere of action, e.g., violence) map onto the SAO linguistic structure of a story grammar, with actors doing certain actions, pro or against other actors.

   (b) Event history analysis and sequence analysis take advantage of other fundamental features of narrative: the timing and duration of actions/events and the sequential organization of the SAO skeleton narrative sentences.

   (c) GIS provides ideal tools for taking advantage of both narrative time and space, allowing us to map the spatiotemporal diffusion of social action (who did what, when, and where).

4. Reliance on statistical techniques that privilege social actors and social action shifts the focus of explanation from variables to actors.

5. Be aware that different rules of well-formedness under different systems of signs (e.g., words in a narrative document and those same

words stored in a relational database) may require the appropriate manipulation of words in a computer environment.

6. Be also aware that the narrative richness of narrative analysis is deceptive; events occur in the context of other events; to understand the events of interest to you (let's say, fascist violence), you need information on these other events, *regardless of the richness of information on the events of specific interest to you*; you need covariates—covariates unlikely to be part of your data collection using a story grammar (e.g., unemployment rate, price indices, electoral returns).

7. Last but not least, be aware that the numbers extracted from words must be put back into words to make sense of them: from words to numbers and back to words. And since in QNA the words are right below the surface of the numbers, use this close relationship between numbers and words when it comes to data analysis and to writing (as the qualitative scholars, discussed in Chapter 2, would recommend).

Notes

1. Wada constructs a 5×5 network matrix based on five claim spheres as nodes, rather than actors (Wada, 2004, p. 248): civic, socioeconomic, economic, political, social.

2. The graphs of Figures 4.5, 4.6, and 4.7 are based on a square root transformation of the raw data to make the thickness of the lines comparable across graphs.

3. Section written with Ivano Bison.

4. For classic references on spectral analysis, see Box and Jenkins (1970); on ARIMA models, see Jenkins and Watts (1968); on event history analysis, see Allison (1984).

5. Section written with Ivano Bison.

6. For a critique of this aspect of Propp's morphology of stories, see Bremond (1966). Bremond argues that stories are not all characterized by a single invariant macrostructural sequence. Rather, invariant sequences are characteristic of microstructures (i.e., parts of stories), and those sequentially invariant microstructures combine in a multiplicity of ever-varying ways to form complex narrative macrostructures.

7. Maranda's DISCAN program was used; Pierre Maranda and Sylvie Nadeau, 1990, DISCAN: Package for Automatic Content and Discourse Analysis. User's Manual.

8. Section written with Claude Rubinson.

9. On these issues, see Franzosi (2004b, pp. 314–318); see also Alexander and Giesen (1987, p. 17); on the general theoretical problem of the micro-macro link, see the articles in Alexander, Giesen, Münch, and Smelser (1987).

10. The labels are self-explanatory, but beautification refers to the types of activities intended to enhance a character's appearance (e.g., a visit to the hairdresser or hours spent in front of a mirror), and emotions can be either positive or negative. Given the nature of the activities, the same activity can be coded several times (e.g., a leisure activity can also be an interaction).

11. Technically, these types of problems are known as "anaphora resolution" problems.

12. In PC-ACE, users code an object (e.g., an actor with all its characteristics), and every time the object is used in different triplets, they establish a direct link to that original object rather than code the object anew. This not only saves coding time but insures that a computer will link the same object, let's say, an actor (and not a generic actor but *that* specific actor), to some actions.

13. Imagine the case of having coded two different locations for <space> for two different semantic triplets within the same event. Which location should a routine choose for imputing <space> automatically to all triplets?

CHAPTER 5. CODA

From Words to Numbers, From Numbers to Words

We have come to the end of our journey. Starting from words and crossing different disciplines—namely, linguistics, computer science, and statistics—we have extracted numbers from the comparative analysis of narratives, and on those numbers we have applied tools that allow us to highlight patterns *hidden* behind the individual narratives. But patterns and numbers don't speak for themselves. They too have to be interpreted, put back into words. Even current social science journal articles are not made up of tables, graphs, and equations alone. A picture may be worth a thousand words, but the network, sequence, event history, and GIS pictures (Figures 4.5 through 4.13) *still* needed words of explanation. The words have the last word.

Systems of Signs and Logics of Explanation

There is quite a difference between the regression model of Equation 4.1 (see p. 107), meant to test the red menace hypothesis, and the prototypical example of fascist violence as described in the Lucca Labor Chamber story (see p. 1) that Equation 4.1 attempts to explain: Not only do they look physically different as system of signs—a collection of mathematical symbols and numbers versus a collection of words—but they interpret and represent social reality in different terms, in terms of variables and in terms of social actors and their actions (in time and space). Signs, of course, are meaningful in relation to other signs. Understanding a story requires linguistic competence, perhaps historical and social knowledge of a period, a country. Equation 4.1 requires knowledge of mathematics and statistics.

The two systems of signs are vulnerable to different problems: The story system of signs is vulnerable to problems of semantic coherence, syntactical sentence well-formedness, and rhetorical persuasiveness; the system of signs of Equations 4.1 and 4.2, to problems of estimating methods, disposition of the data points in the regression space (in terms of outliers and influential observations), and correlated error terms (e.g., see Franzosi, 1994a).

They direct our attention to different worlds: actors and their actions in a story and variables in the statistical/mathematical model.

They have different premises. A story would ideally be as rich as possible, with as much information as possible about an event. Equation 4.1 ideally wants to be as "parsimonious" as possible, explain a dependent variable in terms of as few independent variables as possible. "Whole" versus "model" approaches to sociohistorical explanation, Goethe versus Newton, clash here (see Franzosi, forthcoming).

Finally, they have different logics of explanations. Stories are interested in social action, in who does what, when, and where and for what reasons and with what consequences. The sequential organization of stories may provide causal arguments and justifications. In Equations 1 and 2, the interest is in the effect on a "dependent" variable (Y) of a given "independent" variable X_j (with j varying from 1 to k, the number of "independent" variables). The questions change: What happens to variable Y when variable X_j goes up or down? Will Y also go up? By how much? How will the interaction between the variables X_1 and X_2 affect Y? In these representations, social actors, "the agents of history . . . are nowhere to be seen," as Braudel wrote, or, to say it with Perrot, it is easy to forget that "there are people behind numbers" (cited in Franzosi, 2004b, pp. 240–241).

With text data organized in the SAO storylike structure and their homologous representations in network and other models, agency and social action are never forgotten (on these issues, see Abell, 2004; Franzosi, 2004b, pp. 240–242). All the statistical analyses based on QNA data made one thing clear: the role of social actors and social actions in bringing about a fascist outcome at the end of the period from 1919 to 1922. This way, perhaps, quantitative narrative analysis and the statistical tools it maps onto lead to a rapprochement of history and the social sciences (see Franzosi, 2004b, pp. 247–252).

Text and Con.text (Beyond Questions For/From a Story)

In variable-based statistical explanations, a "dependent" variable (typically event counts in sociohistorical research, e.g., the yearly number of lynching events or of strikes) is "explained" as a function of a set of "independent" variables (e.g., the price of cotton and the black/white racial ratio in a county/year in lynching models or the unemployment rate and political party in power per year/quarter and country in strike models). Multivariate statistical models build causality by linking a dependent variable to a set of independent, explanatory variables.

In quantitative narrative analysis, the very richness of the available data may lead to a purely descriptive approach to social scientific explanations, instead of a causal one based on a set of explanatory variables (on these issues, see also Franzosi, 2004b, pp. 238–240). The network or event history models presented in this chapter are not related to other characteristics of the social-historical period in which the stories are embedded. The con.texts of those texts (i.e., *con,* what goes *with* the text; Latin *cum* = with) are lost. The rich stories of those models do not tell us anything about the worsening economic conditions (in terms of rising inflation and unemployment by the end of 1920, not just in Italy but across Europe) or anything about the electoral victories of the Socialist Party at the administrative election of November 1920 and political elections of May 1921.[1] Our focus on stories of social conflict and political violence has been selective. There are myriad other events that make up social reality and that would tell stories of their own. To put it in Braudel's (1980, p. 67) words, "[A]n event . . . [occurs] within the context of a whole family of other events." Those other events (and their stories) have been left out in my data collection. This is fairly typical in this type of research. But the relationship of these other stories to my stories of social conflict and political violence must *somehow* be teased out (either as stories in their own right with the use of a QNA approach—but the cost of focusing on *all* stories would be prohibitive—or as numbers that represent the aggregate result of those stories, e.g., unemployment rate).

Yet the basic outline of our network, event history, or GIS stories can be greatly enriched while still remaining *within* the realm of our stories. You can combine GIS with network models, focusing on different regions. You can trace the spatiotemporal diffusion of fascist violence in relation to specific networks of social relations as traced by network models. In the *Avanti!* database, we have collected events such as the founding of new local sections of the Fascist Party. Do such events precede or follow violence, or do they occur in areas of no violence? Description can go a long way in providing explanation (and narrative, after all, is a form of explanation in its own right), or, at least, it can raise questions that lead to explanation.

Tricks of the Trade (Parting Recommendations)

It is dissertation time, after a few years of courses. You have been a good student, through hard work, doing well in your courses. You have taken a range of courses on offer, from methods to statistics, from substantive courses to theory. It is now time to put it all together. You are on your own. It won't take long before you realize that you are ill prepared to confront the practice of social research. No one has taught you the tricks of the trade (Becker, 1998). That is true even if you are a seasoned researcher, but you are stepping out of your field of expertise, approaching new problems and new techniques. Every new method and problem has its bag of tricks. What should this bag contain when it comes to quantitative narrative analysis? Here is a helpful list.

146

Start From Your Research Question!
The Telescope and the Microscope

Narrative is many different things, from macrostructures (Propp's, Greimas's, and Colby's functions or Labov's functional parts of narrative) to microstructures (the SAO) and their sequential organization in story and plot (the story grammar). These different "structures" have all been sold in this book as "invariant," and yet they are all different from each other. The point is, *different questions, different structures, different meanings, different measures*. The SAO structure I relied on in my work reflected my original substantive and theoretical interest in the unfolding of sociohistorical processes, my search for the actors. I was interested in what social actors *do* in time and space. I was less interested in forms of representation, in discourse, in the rhetorical and ideological aspects of texts. What I found at the end of the road of my drive toward the quantification of meaning, in light of my specific questions about the behavior of social actors, ultimately reflected what I was looking for. Had I been interested in discourse, I would have found different linguistic structures, different processes of measurement.

Not that the SAO structure is void of rhetorical or ideological aspects. The actors and actions a writer chooses to represent and the actions imputed to different actors involve authorial choices, a differential use of silence and emphasis, representational strategies akin to ideological production (Franzosi, 1998a; 2004b, pp. 147–154, 175–177). Trew (1979a) has shown how not only the choice of words (e.g., terrorist vs. freedom fighter or martyr) but the syntactical structure adopted (e.g., passive vs. active) has profound (ideological) implications in the production of meaning. Even the typographic layout of newspaper articles across the page has ideological effects (Trew, 1979b). And, of course, the work by sociolinguists has shown the existence of a gendered language (e.g., Coates, 1983/1993; Lakoff, 1975; Tannen, 1994) or of racially based language (e.g., Bucholtz, 1999; Smitherman, 1994) and has teased out their characteristics.

Which structures you use, then, and which processes of measurement you adopt depend on what you want to see in the end and, ultimately, on the research question(s) you pose. There is no single research tool that allows you to see everything, micro- and macrostructures (microscope and telescope), syntax and semantics, grammar and rhetoric, factual and ideological aspects of texts (but even a language of facticity is, in itself, already an ideological choice; see Tuchman, 1972). Ask your research questions, first, and take it from there.

Get to Know Your Documents

Your research question will suggest the kind of documents to use for empirical evidence (from newspapers to police reports, Web sites, blogs, diaries, children's books; but familiarity with some documents may well suggest a research question, in the sociological tradition of grounded theory or of a historian's work in the archives). Take a sample of these documents (no need to produce a random sample; just try to get a variety of your source documents). Read each document in your sample, repeatedly. Become very familiar with both content and form, with the structure of language it uses and what it talks about. Train your eye to discern purely narrative passages from descriptive and evaluative or analytical ones. Constantly ask yourself the question "Does this passage, this particular piece of information, fit into my story grammar?"

While reading your documents, particularly when you first approach them (after a while things become familiar and no longer catch your attention), write down anything that strikes you, for whatever reason (suggested relationships, points where the grammar needs tweaking to meet your project's needs, why particular pieces of information seem worth coding and what you would need them for). Pay attention to how your documents structure stories. Does each document typically narrate one story or different and unrelated stories (imagine, for instance, a newspaper article that under the same heading of a strike, reports different and independent strikes occurring at some place and time)? Are the events of a story typically narrated in one document or across several documents over time (e.g., archival, police records of an uprising)? In these documents, what is the mixture of narration, evaluation, and description? Different answers to each of these questions entail perhaps different research designs (in particular, different coding scheme designs) and different forms of organization of the coding task.

And Know Your Coders (The Intercoder Reliability Problem)

Know your documents, no doubt. But also know your coders. Writing during the early stages of development of the technique of content analysis, Lasswell (1942, p. 19) was well aware that "within any given set of symbol categories results depend upon technical coding operations" and that these technical operations concern both the design of coding categories and the role of coders. Coding categories "exercise the most fundamental influence on results," he wrote (p. 19), or, as Berelson (1952) later put it with an expression that would become popular, "content analysis stands or falls by its categories" (p. 147). Coders themselves, standing between text and coding categories, exercise a fundamental role in fitting text into categories. Seemingly technical coding "operations require judgments of meanings . . . Such judgments may be in error" (Janis, 1949, p. 81). As a way out of intractable issues of interpretation and meaning, early developers of the technique recommended "intensive training of the analysts . . . detailed rules of classification," and a focus on surface, rather than latent, meanings.

The latter "is an interpretation," Lasswell wrote (1941, p. 2). They further recommended computing coefficients of intercoder reliability based on the results obtained by different coders reading and coding the same text.

Yet, for all their recommendations (in refrains still very popular today), early developers may have been overly optimistic in their scientific zeal. Our ability to understand even the simplest of texts depends on both contextual and wider knowledge of the "world"—not to mention knowledge of even how to read specific kinds of texts, a code or frame of reference—that goes well beyond what handbooks of coding instructions or training sessions can accomplish.[2] In fact, these palliatives may accomplish no more than a temporary and precarious consensus on coding rules in a team of coders—a consensus to be broken by every new team member, every new team (see Franzosi, 2008, p. xii). "No knowledge without foreknowledge," hermeneutic scholars maintain (Diesing, 1991, p. 108). In the "hermeneutic circle," text comprehension and meaning are constructed in an iterative process where a reader approaches a text with some hypotheses in mind of what the text is all about, looks for clues in the text about those hypotheses, sets up new hypotheses about what the text means, and restarts the reading process.[3] Furthermore, texts are typically not "closed," locking the reader into a preferred reading to the exclusion of all others.[4] Readers come to a text with their own preferences and points of view and read and interpret a text in light of these individual preferences. Eco (1979, p. 4) writes, "The reader as an active principle of interpretation is a part of the picture of the generative process of the text." But if handbooks of coding instructions and training sessions may ultimately fail in "closing" a text into an exclusive and preferential reading, they no doubt succeed in appeasing content analysts' conscience about doing science.

One of the Renaissance master rhetoricians, Erasmus of Rotterdam, in his *Copia: Foundations of the Abundant Style*, first published in 1512, an immensely popular rhetorical textbook, illustrates 147 variations of the sentence, "Your letter pleased me greatly" (*tuae litterae me magnopere delectarunt*). And if that is true for a simple sentence of only five words, I leave it to your imagination to think of how many different ways there are for coders to interpret, parse, and assign the various textual elements of the several sentences that make up a story to the categories of a story grammar. There will no doubt be differences; there will be "some" problems of intercoder reliability.

Awareness of the role of the reader may put the problems of intercoder reliability in a more realistic perspective. But it may also help researchers organize the coding task. A Tayloristic approach to coding, where different coders are involved in coding different parts of a text, may not be the most reliable (and perhaps not even the most efficient) (e.g., Tilly, 1995). Text understanding requires a reader's continuous involvement with the text, with all parts of a text (and even its context). Breaking up coding would *still* require a *full* understanding of the text by each coder. Consider two- or even multiple-pass coding, instead of the more tempting one-pass coding (see p. 59).

Work Backward

OK. You now have a bag full of tricks, and you are, no doubt, ready and eager to put them into practice. Don't be impatient. I have one more piece of advice for you: Be realistic! Content analysis is a very labor-intensive process, even with the help of specialized computer software (truly indispensable for large projects).

What does it mean to be realistic? Simple. Ask yourself the following questions: How much time do I have? How much money? Compute how much time different types of coding schemes require for coding (you get faster with time, but don't expect miracles; after a while, coding time stays pretty constant; budget 10 to 15 minutes per one-page document for an experienced coder working with a fairly complex coding scheme yielding 10 or so triplets per document). In which medium are your documents? Microfilms? Printed material? Computer files? Does your software require computer documents? If so, but your documents are on microfilms or in print form, you will need to scan them in and convert them to computer files (not a pain-free task). If you rely on others to do the coding for you (employing a team of coders on a funded research project), remember this: Coding is not for everyone. Repetitive work that requires careful attention and intelligence don't go hand in hand. Plan to train 10 coders and, if lucky, you may end up with 5. Once you have estimated the coding time that each document takes, you will have an idea of how many documents you can code within your budget (and/or time). If necessary, sample! But you may also wish to consider narrowing down your problem, refining your questions, streamlining your coding scheme. The Hubble telescope delivers infinitely more information than did the 6× and 20× telescopes that Galileo had at his disposal. But it also requires far more complex and sophisticated technology for handling information. Complex coding schemes not only entail more time-consuming data entry (coding) but also more time-consuming and more sophisticated forms of data analysis. Remember: The most brilliant research question will remain unanswered if you have run out of time or money along the way.

Consider Sampling

In one of the early methodological papers on content analysis written in 1943, Alexander Mintz (1943/1949), then a researcher in Lasswell's Experimental Division for the Study of War Time Communications, recommended "sampling of the (input) material as a labor-saving device" when this material "involves a large number of items" and coding would take "much time and labor." (p. 127) That recommendation has been repeated (and followed) by most content analysis investigators. At the very least, sampling involves selecting the time frame for the documents to be analyzed (e.g., 1919–1922) and the data sources (e.g., specific newspapers, magazines, Web sites). All content analysis projects are based on such a sampling frame. Some projects also sample *within* these frames. They select randomly one magazine issue per month or five per year. They restrict the material to foreign news or to the home page of Web sites. Even in research projects where investigators are interested not in forms of representations (e.g., content analysis of advertisements and commercials or of media bias in the news) but in people's behavior in the protest event analysis tradition, they restrict their sample to specific days of the week or random months.[5] They restrict their focus to certain key events (e.g., political elections) and systematically collect data "around" those events (e.g., Wada, 2004). They sample pages, paragraphs, or sentences within documents (e.g., Doyle, 2009; Gross, Harmon, & Reidy, 2002, pp. 10–12, 235–242). Sampling can be applied to reduce not only the amount of material to be analyzed in input but also that of coded output, perhaps applying acceptance sampling schemes that insure predefined standards of quality at lower costs (Franzosi, 2004b, pp. 78–79).

Sampling would be particularly recommended if you decide to code linguistic or nonnarrative elements of your documents (description, evaluation, themes/conceptual space, rhetoric). You do not need thousands of documents to highlight linguistic features of documents and/or ideological differences between documents. The analyses I carried out on two articles from a left-wing newspaper and a right-wing one clearly showed the ideological biases of the two newspapers (Franzosi, 2004a). A good sampling framework may be an appropriate strategy in these cases. Such, for instance, is the strategy adopted by Gross et al. (2002) to study the rhetorical structure of social science journal articles. Such is the strategy typically adopted by most content analysis research projects (Franzosi, 2008). But if the study of what happened in history is at stake (e.g., if you use archival documents or newspaper articles to study historical events rather than the way these events may be represented), sampling may be more problematic. You may end up missing out on "history as it actually happened," in the famous words of von Ranke—the father of modern historiography—leaving events out, chopping actors or actions out of events (a problem known as "censoring" in statistics). Yet, even in these cases, sampling of documents has been adopted as a research strategy (on these issues, see Franzosi, 2004b, pp. 73–74, 78–79).

So sample, by all means, to make a research project manageable, but be aware of the consequences! Be also aware of the fact that no documents we use (including von Ranke's Venetian ambassadorial reports—*relazioni*—Franzosi, 2004b, 183–187) ever give a full picture of sociohistorical reality. They themselves will have filtered that reality for you, will have selected events, actors, and actions before your own sampling framework. And while you know and control the parameters of your own sampling strategy, that of the actors (individual or institutional) who produced those documents is out of your hands. Make an effort to shine some light on the selection strategies of the producers of those documents!

Sampling (The Other Way Around)

The sampling strategies outlined above aim at reducing the size and costs of a project. A different type of sampling strategy would go in the opposite direction, sampling coded documents or coded events for more in-depth investigations (but the two strategies are not mutually exclusive). You could sample documents to gain deeper insights into both language and social relations of your documents through, for instance, qualitative narrative analysis (Franzosi, 1998a; Kohler Riessman, 1993). Even the 17th-century Linceans, for all their misgivings about the role of detailed pictures of the natural world in the advancement of science, accepted their role in suggesting relations among things (see Freedberg, 2002, pp. 7–8). Similarly, you could sample events for a more in-depth historical or statistical investigation (e.g., through Ragin's Qualitative Comparative Analysis).

Where Should You Put Your Money? Reliability Versus Validity

"Content analysts have been rather casual about validating their results," Krippendorf (1980, p. 155) wrote in his classic book, *Content Analysis* (1980). Indeed, their obsession has always rather been reliability since it affects one of the main tenets of science: reproducibility of findings (different coders using the same measurement instrument on the same material should obtain the same results). Yet, in the early days of the development of the technique, Janis (1949, pp. 56–57) had already asked, "Let us assume that we have tested the reliability of a content-analysis technique. . . . The question then arises: *What do the content-analysis results describe?*" Do your empirical results really address your theoretical constructs? Is it media bias that your coding categories tap, or is it something else? Janis's question is particularly salient if you are using content analysis (or quantitative narrative analysis) for historical research. As I put it (Franzosi, 2004b),

What is the point of making sure that a figure of 200,000 for the size of a crowd is properly recorded, when such a figure may actually verge on the fantastic and when, furthermore, there is an equal likelihood of it being overestimated or underestimated? Given that nonrandom error (validity) is much more likely to distort historical data than random error (reliability) and given the disproportionate attention paid to problems of reliability than of validity, I would recommend a shift in focus from problems of reliability to problems of validity. (pp. 182–183)

If you are doing historical research, how can you be sure that the direction of the violence between fascists and socialists (as measured by network models) is not the result of using a socialist newspaper? If you are using Web blogs to make arguments about gendered language and you are linking specific forms of discourse to specific genders, how can you validate the real gender of an anonymous blogger? Don't bark up the wrong tree! Allocate some of your research funds to address issues of validity (e.g., collecting data from different sources).

From Theory to Method, From Method to Theory

A simple quest pushed me along this journey from words to numbers: a search for the actor, motivated by a substantive/theoretical view of social reality (and history) where actors and their actions, rather than variables, play fundamental roles. That view forced me to break new methodological ground, as described in these pages. But those new methods (of rewrite rules and relations) forced, in their turn, a new substantive/theoretical vision of sociology (and the social sciences in general) as *social relations,* to which Marx, Weber, and Simmel contributed (on these broader issues, see Franzosi, 2004b, pp. 237–273). Theory and method never stray too far from each other.

Words and Numbers (Quality and Quantity), Awe, and Humility

For all the advantages of quantification, be well aware of its shortcomings, of which there are many. In the realm of numbers, it is easy to forget where numbers come from in content analysis (including quantitative narrative analysis): from words, as found in texts and in coding schemes. Meaning and interpretation—so crucial in the realm of words—fall in the background as objectivity and science are foregrounded. The role of the reader or of coding scheme design is forgotten. Content analysts' use of a language of science through a relentless focus on methodological issues (sampling, recording units, pretesting of coding categories, coefficients of intercoder reliability) has successfully diverted attention from the most intractable problems of content analysis: the role of the reader. And that role certainly does not disappear even in quantitative narrative analysis, although the reader/coder may be involved in a more natural process of understanding stories and placing the elements of a story within more familiar categories of *who* does *what, when, where, why,* and *how.*

In quantitative narrative analysis, the words are right below the surface where the numbers rest, always only one click away from the numbers. Turn this property to your advantage. Bring up those words and use them not simply as sound bytes, but (1) to provide con.text to your numbers, (2) to suggest relations, following the clues offered by words (see Franzosi, 1998a), and (3) to reinforce the explanatory logic of quantitative narrative analysis, actor based rather than variable based. It should not be words *versus* numbers, quality *versus* quantity, but words *and* numbers, quality *and* quantity. Count and recount, measure and narrate; numbers and words, share the same etymological root based on the sequential organization of narrative (Franzosi, 2004b, p. 32).

In the end, out of the combination of different research questions that lead to different measurement strategies and, no doubt, errors of both omission and commission (across and *within* coders, during data entry and data aggregation), you will have fashioned a peculiar research object. You will have done your best to catch these errors through ongoing monitoring of data quality (verification for semantic coherence and input vs. output) and through data cleaning, during and after the completion of data collection. But some errors will slip through. Approach this object with the awe of someone aware of having fashioned something new and beautiful, but also approach it with the humility of someone aware of being involved in both science and alchemy (or at least art, and that's the beauty). The issue is not one of giving up on the pursuit of a rigorous approach to social science and even less so of a postmodern attitude where "anything flies" because, in any case, there is "no reality out there." The issue is one of pursuing an honest approach to science that acknowledges all its (many) limitations. And with a bit of luck, you may even be able to say something meaningful about sociohistorical reality. So—good luck!

Notes

1. On the limits of covariates for narrative type data, see Koopmans and Statham (1999, pp. 205–206) and Franzosi (2004b, pp. 238–240).

2. Barthes in his S/Z (1990) uses the concept of "code," while Eco (1979) talks about "intertextual frames" (pp. 5, 7, 208); and Perry (1979, p. 36) about "frames."

3. On the "hermeneutic circle," see Diesing (1991, pp. 109, 121). On the text and its reading, see also Rimmon-Kenan (1983, pp. 117–129, in particular 119–122) and Cohan and Shires (1988, pp. 114–133). On the dynamic of text reading as a system of hypotheses, see Perry (1979, p. 43), Culler (1975), and de Beaugrande (1982).

4. On "open" and "closed" texts, see Eco (1979, pp. 8–11).

5. For several references to scholarly reliance on the Monday issues of newspapers, see Franzosi (2004b, p. 73).

REFERENCES

Abbott, A. (1995). Sequence analysis: New methods for old ideas. *Annual Review of Sociology, 21,* 93–113.

Abbott, A., & Barman, E. (1997). Sequence comparison via alignment and Gibbs sampling: A formal analysis of the emergence of the modern sociological article. In A. E. Raftery (Ed.), *Sociological methodology* (Vol. 27, pp. 47–87). Oxford, UK: Blackwell.

Abbott, A., & Alexandra, H. (1990). Measuring resemblance in sequence data. *American Journal of Sociology, 96,* 144–185.

Abbott, A., & Hrycak, A. (1990). Measuring resemblance in sequence data. *American Journal of Sociology, 96,* 144–185.

Abell, P. (1987). *The syntax of social life: The theory and method of comparative narratives.* Oxford, UK: Clarendon Press.

Abell, P. (1993). Some aspects of narrative method [Special issue]. *Journal of Mathematical Sociology, 18*(2/3), 93–134.

Abell, P. (2004). Narrative explanation: An alternative to variable-centered explanation? *Annual Review of Sociology, 30,* 287–310.

Alexa, M., & Zuell, C. (2000). Text analysis software: Commonalities, differences and limitations: The results of a review. *Quality & Quantity, 34*(3), 299–321.

Alexander, J. C., & Giesen, B. (1987). From reduction to linkage: The long view of the micro-macro debate. In J. C. Alexander, B. Giesen, R. Münch, & N. J. Smelser (Eds.), *The micro-macro link* (pp. 1–42). Berkeley: University of California Press.

Alexander, J. C., Giesen, B., Münch, R., & Smelser, N. J. (Eds.). (1987). *The micro-macro link.* Berkeley: University of California Press.

Allison, P. D. (1984). *Event history analysis: Regression for longitudinal event data.* Beverly Hills, CA: Sage.

Austin, J. L. (1975). *How to do things with words* (J. O. Urmson & Marina Sbisà, Eds.) (2nd ed.). Cambridge, MA: Harvard University Press. (Original work published 1962)

Bailyn, B. (1982). The challenge of modern historiography. *American Historical Review, 87*(1), 1–24.

Bal, M. (1977). *Narratologie: Essais sur la signification narrative dans quatre romans modernes* [Narratology: Essays on the narrative signification in four modern novels]. Paris: Editions Klincksieck.

Barthes, R. (1977). Introduction to the structural analysis of narratives. In R. Barthes (Ed.), & S. Heath (Trans.), *Image music text* (pp. 79–124). London: Fontana Press. (Original work published 1966)

Barthes, R. (1990). *S/Z.* Oxford, UK: Blackwell. (Original work published 1970)

Bearman, P. S., & Stovel, K. (2000). Becoming a Nazi: Models for narrative networks. *Poetics, 27*(2/3), 69–90.

de Beaugrande, R. (1982). The story of grammars and the grammar of stories. *Journal of Pragmatics, 6*(5/6), 383–422.

155

Becker, H. S. (1963). *Outsiders: Studies in the sociology of deviance*. New York: Free Press.
Becker, H. S. (1998). *Tricks of the trade: How to think about your research while you're doing it*. Chicago: University of Chicago Press.
Bell, D. H. (1986). *Sesto San Giovanni: Workers, culture and politics in an Italian town, 1880–1922*. New Brunswick, NJ: Rutgers University Press.
Benford, R. D., & Snow, D. A. (2000). Framing processes and social movements: An overview and assessment. *Annual Review of Sociology, 26,* 611–639.
Benveniste, E. (1971). *Problems in general linguistics*. Coral Gables, FL: University of Miami Press. (Original work published 1966)
Berelson, B. (1952). *Content analysis in communication research*. Glencoe, IL: Free Press.
Berg, B. L. (2004). *Qualitative research methods for the social sciences* (5th ed.). Boston: Pearson.
Bison, I. (2009). Lexicographic index: A new measurement of resemblance among sequences. In M. Williams & P. Vogt (Eds.), *Handbook of methodological innovations in the social sciences*. Thousand Oaks, CA: Sage.
Blossfeld, H.P., & Rohwer, G. (1995). *Techniques of event history modeling: New approaches to causal analysis*. Hillsdale, NJ: Lawrence Erlbaum.
Bond, D., Jenkins, J. C., Taylor, C. L., & Schock, K. (1997). Mapping mass political conflict and civil society: Issues and prospects for the automated development of event data. *Journal of Conflict Resolution, 41*(4), 553–579.
Bond, D., Bond, J., Oh, C., Jenkins, J. C., & Taylor, C. L. (2003). Integrated Data for Events Analysis (IDEA): An event typology for automated events data development. *Journal of Peace Research, 40*(6), 733–745.
Box, G., & Jenkins, G. (1970). *Time series analysis: Forecasting and control*. San Francisco: Holden-Day.
Braudel, F. (1980). *On history*. Chicago: University of Chicago Press.
Bremond, C. (1966). La logique des possibles narratives [The logic of narrative possibilities]. *Communications, 8,* 60–76.
Brustein, W. (1991). The red menace and the rise of Italian fascism. *American Sociological Review, 56,* 652–664.
Bucholtz, M. (1999). You da Man: Narrating the racial other in the production of white masculinity. *Journal of Sociolinguistics, 3*(4), 443–460.
Burke, K. (1969). *A grammar of motives*. Berkeley: University of California Press. (Original work published 1945)
Carley, K. (1993). Coding choices for textual analysis: A comparison of content analysis and map analysis. In P. Marsden (Ed.), *Sociological methodology* (Vol. 23, pp. 75–126). Oxford, UK: Blackwell.
Carley, K. (1994). Extracting culture through textual analysis. *Poetics, 22*(4), 291–312.
Charlesworth, A. (1979). *Social protest in a rural society: The spatial diffusion of the captain swing disturbances of 1830–1831* (Historical Geography Research Series 1). Norwich, UK: Geo Abstracts, University of East Anglia.
Chatman, S. (1978). *Story and discourse: Narrative structure in fiction and film*. Ithaca, NY: Cornell University Press.
Clifford, J., & Marcus, G. E. (Eds.). (1986). *Writing culture: The poetics and politics of ethnography*. Berkeley: University of California Press.
Coates, J. (1993). *Women, man and language* (2nd ed.). London: Longman. (Original work published 1983)
Cohan, S., & Shires, L. M. (1988). *Telling stories: A theoretical analysis of narrative fiction*. New York: Routledge.

156

Colarizi, S. (1977). *Dopoguerra e fascismo in Puglia, 1919/1926* [War aftermath and fascism in Apulia, 1919/1926]. Bari, Italy: Laterza.

Colby, B. N. (1973). A partial grammar of Eskimo folktales. *American Anthropologist, 75*(3), 645–662.

Corner, P. (1975). *Fascism in Ferrara, 1915–1925.* Oxford, UK: Oxford University Press.

Corsaro, W., & Heise, D. (1990). Event structure models from ethnographic data. In C. C. Clogg (Ed.), *Sociological methodology* (Vol. 20, pp. 1–57). Oxford, UK: Blackwell.

Culler, J. (1975). *Structuralist poetics: Structuralism, linguistics, and the study of literature.* London: Routledge & Kegan Paul.

Danto, A. C. (1985). *Narration and knowledge.* New York: Columbia University Press.

Date, C. J. (1981). *An introduction to database systems.* Reading, MA: Addison Wesley.

Date, C. J. (1987). *A guide to the SQL standard.* Reading, MA: Addison Wesley.

De Felice, R. (1969). *Le interpretazioni del Fascismo* [Interpretations of fascism]. Bari, Italy: Laterza.

Denzin, N. K., & Lincoln, Y. S. (Eds.). (2005). *The Sage handbook of qualitative research* (3rd ed.). Thousand Oaks, CA: Sage.

Denzin, N. K., & Lincoln, Y. S. (Eds.). (1994). *Handbook of qualitative research.* Thousand Oaks, CA: Sage.

DeVault, M. L. (1991). *Feeding the family. The social organization of caring as gendered work.* Chicago: University of Chicago Press.

Diesner, J., & Carley, K. (2004). *AutoMap1.2: Extract, analyze, represent, and compare mental models from texts* (CASOS Technical Report). Pittsburgh, PA: Carnegie Mellon University, Institute for Software Research International.

Diesing, P. (1991). *How does social science work? Reflections on practice.* Pittsburgh, PA: University of Pittsburgh Press.

Dietrich, S. W. (2001). *Understanding relational database query languages.* Upper Saddle River, NJ: Prentice Hall.

Doyle, S. (2009). *"The stories most of all": A content analysis of bestselling children's books in Britain (1964–2004).* (Doctoral dissertation, University of Oxford, UK, 2009).

Dwyer, K. (1982). *Moroccan dialogues: Anthropology in question.* Baltimore: Johns Hopkins University Press.

Eco, U. (1979). *The role of the reader: Explorations in the semiotics of texts.* Bloomington: Indiana University Press.

Edmondson, R. (1984). *Rhetoric in sociology.* London: Macmillan.

Elliott, J. (2005). *Using narrative in social research: Qualitative and quantitative approaches.* Thousand Oaks, CA: Sage.

Elmasri, R., & Navathe, S. B. (2006). *Fundamentals of database systems.* Reading, MA: Addison Wesley.

Ericsson, K. A., & Simon, H. (1996). *Protocol analysis: Verbal reports as data* (2nd ed.). Cambridge: MIT Press.

Fararo, T. J. (1993). Generating narrative forms. *Journal of Mathematical Sociology, 18*(2/3), 153–181.

Fararo, T. J., & Skvoretz, J. (1986). Action and institution, network and function: The cybernetic concept of social structure. *Sociological Forum, 1*(2), 219–250.

Feagin, J. R., & Sikes, M. P. (1994). *Living with racism: The black middle-class experience.* Boston: Beacon Press.

Franzosi, R. (1989). From words to numbers: A generalized and linguistics-based coding procedure for collecting event-data from newspapers. In C. Clogg (Ed.), *Sociological methodology* (Vol. 19, pp. 263–298). Oxford, UK: Basil Blackwell.

Franzosi, R. (1994a). From words to numbers: A set theory framework for the collection, organization, and analysis of narrative data. In P. Marsden (Ed.), *Sociological methodology* (Vol. 24, pp. 105–136). Oxford, UK: Basil Blackwell.

Franzosi, R. (1994b). Outside and inside the regression black box: A new approach to data analysis. *Quality and Quantity, 28,* 21–53.

Franzosi, R. (1995). *The puzzle of strikes: Class and state strategies in postwar Italy.* Cambridge, UK: Cambridge University Press.

Franzosi, R. (1997). Mobilization and counter-mobilization processes: From the "Red Years" (1919–20) to the "Black Years" (1921–22) in Italy [Special double issue on New Directions in Formalization and Historical Analysis]. *Theory and Society, 26*(2/3), 275–304.

Franzosi, R. (1998a). Narrative analysis: Why (and how) sociologists should be interested in narrative. In J. Hagan (Ed.), *The annual review of sociology* (pp. 517–554). Palo Alto, CA: Annual Reviews.

Franzosi, R. (1998b). Narrative as data: Linguistic and statistical tools for the quantitative study of historical events. *International Review of Social History, 43,* 81–104.

Franzosi, R. (1999). The return of the actor: Networks of interactions among social actors during periods of high mobilization (Italy, 1919–22). *Mobilization, 4*(2), 131–149.

Franzosi, R. (2004a). Content analysis. In A. Bryman & M. Hardy (Eds.), *Handbook of data analysis* (pp. 547–566). Thousand Oaks, CA: Sage.

Franzosi, R. (2004b). *From words to numbers: Narrative, data, and social science.* Cambridge, UK: Cambridge University Press.

Franzosi, R. (2008). *Content analysis: Benchmarks in social research methods series* (Quantitative Applications in the Social Sciences, 4 vols.). Thousand Oaks, CA: Sage.

Franzosi, R. (forthcoming). Sociology, narrative, and the quality versus quantity debate (Goethe versus Newton). *Theory and Society.*

Franzosi, R., Doyle, S., McClelland, L., Rankin, C. P., & Vicari, S. (2009). *Quantitative narrative analysis. Software options compared: PC-ACE and CAQDAS (ATLAS.ti, MAXQDA, and NVivo).* Unpublished manuscript.

Franzosi, R., & Cunial, F. (2009). *Database design for quantitative narrative analysis.* Unpublished manuscript.

Freedberg, D. (2002). *The eye of the lynx: Galileo, his friends, and the beginnings of modern natural history.* Chicago: University of Chicago Press.

Gamson, W. A. (1992). *Talking politics.* Cambridge, UK: Cambridge University Press.

Gamson, W. A., & Modigliani, A. (1989). Media discourse and public opinion on nuclear war. *American Journal of Sociology, 95*(1), 1–37.

Genette, G. (1980). *Narrative discourse: An essay in method* (J. E. Lewin, Trans.). Ithaca, NY: Cornell University Press. (Original work published 1972)

Georgia adds another lynching. (1936, April 29). *Atlanta Daily World,* p. 6.

Gibson, D. (2005). Taking turns and talking ties: Network structure and conversational sequences. *American Journal of Sociology, 110*(6), 1561–1597.

Ginzburg, R. (1962). *100 years of lynchings.* Baltimore: Black Classic Press.

Glaser, B. G., & Strauss, A. L. (1967). *The discovery of grounded theory: Strategies for qualitative research.* New York: Aldine.

Greimas, A. J. (1966). *Sémantique structurale.* Paris: Larousse.

Greimas, A. J. (1971). Narrative grammar: Units and levels. *Modern Language Notes, 86,* 793–806.

Grier, D. A. (2005). *When computers were human.* Princeton, NJ: Princeton University Press.

Griffin, L. (1993). Narrative, event-structure analysis, and causal interpretation in historical sociology. *American Journal of Sociology, 98*(5), 1094–1133.

158

Gross, A. G., Harmon, J. E., & Reidy, M. (2002). *Communicating science.* Oxford, UK: Oxford University Press.

Guerin-Pace, F. (1998). Textual statistics: An exploratory tool for the social sciences. *Population: An English Selection, 10*(1):73–95.

Hägerstrand, T. (1967). *Innovation diffusion as a spatial process.* Chicago: University of Chicago Press.

Halliday, M. A. K. (1994). *An introduction to functional grammar.* London: Arnold. (Original work published 1985)

Halliwell, S. (1987). *The Poetics of Aristotle* (Translation and commentary). London: Duckworth.

Hedström, P. (1994). Contagious collectivities: On the spatial diffusion of Swedish trade unions, 1890–1940. *American Journal of Sociology, 99*(5), 1157–1179.

Heise, D. (1989). Modeling event structures. *Journal of Mathematical Sociology, 14,* 139–169.

Heise, D. (1993). Narratives without meaning? *Journal of Mathematical Sociology, 18*(2/3), 183–189.

Holsti, O. (1969). *Content analysis for the social sciences and humanities.* Reading, MA: Addison Wesley.

Janis, I. L. (1949). The problem of validating content analysis. In H. D. Lasswell, N. Leites, & Associates (Eds.), *Language of politics: Studies in quantitative semantics* (pp. 55–82). Cambridge: MIT Press.

Jenkins, G., & Watts, D. (1968). *Spectral analysis and its applications.* San Francisco: Holden-Day.

Katz, E., Gurevitch, M., Danet, B., & Peled, T. (1969). Petitions and prayers: A content analysis of persuasive appeals. *Social Forces, 47*(4), 447–463.

Kennedy, G. (1994). *A new history of classical rhetoric.* Princeton, NJ: Princeton University Press.

Kohler Riessman, C. (1993). *Narrative analysis* (Qualitative research methods series no. 30). Newbury Park, CA: Sage.

Koopmans, R., & Rucht, D. (2002). Protest event analysis. In R. Koopmans & S. Staggenborg (Eds.), *Methods of social movement research* (pp. 231–259). Minneapolis: University of Minnesota Press.

Koopmans, R., & Statham, P. (1999). Political claims analysis: Integrating protest event and political discourse approaches. *Mobilization, 4*(2), 203–221.

Koopmans, R., Statham, P., Giugni, M., & Passy, F. (2005). *Contested citizenship: Immigration and cultural diversity in Europe.* Minneapolis: University of Minnesota Press.

Krippendorf, K. (1980). *Content analysis: An introduction to its methodology.* Beverly Hills, CA: Sage.

Labov, W. (1972). *Language in the inner city.* Philadelphia: University of Pennsylvania Press.

Labov, W. (1973). The boundaries of words and their meanings. In C.-J. N. Bailey & R. W. Shuy (Eds.), *New ways of analyzing variation in English* (pp. 340–373). Washington, DC: Georgetown University Press.

Labov, W., & Waletzky, J. (1967). Narrative analysis. In J. Helm (Ed.), *Essays on the verbal and visual arts* (pp. 12–44). Seattle: University of Washington Press.

Lakoff, R. (1975). *Language and women's place.* New York: Harper Torch Books.

Lanham, R. A. (1991). *A handlist of rhetorical terms.* Berkeley: University of California Press.

Lasswell, H. D. (1938). A provisional classification of symbol data. *Psychiatry: Journal of the Biology and the Pathology of Interpersonal Relations, 1,* 197–204.

Lasswell, H, D. (1942). Analyzing the content of mass communication: A brief introduction. *Experimental Division for the Study of War Time Communications* (Document No. 11). Washington, DC: Library of Congress.

159

Lasswell, H. D. (1949). "Why Be Quantitative?" In: H. D. Lasswell, N. Leites, & Associates. *Language of politics: Studies in quantitative semantics* (pp. 40–52). Cambridge: MIT Press.

Laver, M., Benoit, K., & Garry, J. (2003). Extracting policy positions from political texts using words as data. *American Political Science Review, 97*(2), 311–331.

Lébart, L., Morineau, A., & Bécue, M. (1989). *SPAD T: Système portable pour l'analise des données textuelles* [Portable system for the analysis of textual data]. Paris: CISIA

Lefebvre, G. (1973). *The Great Fear of 1789: Rural panic in revolutionary France*. New York: Pantheon Books. (Original work published 1956)

Levin, B. (1993). *English verb classes and alternations: A preliminary investigation*. Chicago: The University of Chicago Press.

Lewins, A., & Silver, C. (2007). *Using software in qualitative research: A step-by-step guide*. London: Sage.

Leites, N., & de Sola Pool, E. (2008). On content analysis. In R. Franzosi (Ed.), *Content analysis. Benchmarks in social research methods series* (Vol. 1, pp. 140–159) (Quantitative Applications in the Social Sciences, 4 vols). Thousand Oaks, CA: Sage. (Original work published 1942)

Lipset, S. M. (1959). *Political man: The social bases of politics*. Baltimore: Johns Hopkins Press.

Lucca's labor chamber destroyed. (1921, April 1). *Avanti!*, p. 1.

Mandler, J. (1982). Some uses and abuses of a story grammar. *Discourse Processes, 5*(3/4), 305–318.

Mandler, J. M., & Johnson, N. S. (1977). Remembrance of things parsed: Story structure and recall. *Cognitive Psychology, 9*(1), 111–151.

Markoff, J., Shapiro, G., & Weitman, S. (1975). Toward the integration of content analysis and general methodology. In D. R. Heise (Ed.), *Sociological methodology* (Vol. 6, pp. 1–58). San Francisco: Jossey-Bass.

Massey, D. (2005). *For space*. Thousand Oaks, CA: Sage.

Maynes, M. J, Pierce, J. L., & Laslett, B. (2008). *Telling stories: The use of personal narratives in the social sciences and history*. Ithaca, NY: Cornell University Press.

McAdam, D. (1988). *Freedom summer*. Oxford, UK: Oxford University Press.

McCloskey, D. (1985). *The rhetoric of economics*. Madison: University of Wisconsin Press.

Mintz, A. (1949). The feasibility of the use of samples in content analysis. In H. D. Lasswell, N. Leites, & Associates (Eds.), *Language of politics: Studies in quantitative semantics* (pp. 127–152). New York: George W. Stewart (Reprinted from *Content analysis,* Sage Benchmarks in Social Research Methods Series [Quantitative Applications in the Social Sciences, 4 vols], Vol. 1, pp. 159–179, by R. Franzosi, Ed. , 2008, Thousand Oaks, CA: Sage). (Original work published 1943)

Mishler, E. G. (1986). *Research interviewing: Context and narrative*. Cambridge, MA: Harvard University Press.

Moore, B. (1966). *Social origins of dictatorship and democracy: Lord and peasant in the making of the modern world*. Boston: Beacon Press.

Muhr, T., & Friese, S. (2004). *User's manual for ATLAS.ti 5.0* (2nd ed.). Berlin, Germany: Scientific Software Development.

Oliver, P. E., & Myers, D. J. (1999). How events enter the public sphere: Conflict, location, and sponsorship in local newspaper coverage of public events. *American Journal of Sociology, 105*(1), 38–87.

Oxford English Dictionary. (1989). Oxford: Oxford University Press.

Perrot, M. (1968). Grèves, grévistes et conjoncture. Vieux problèmes, travaux neufs [Strikes, strikers and conjuncture: Old problems, new scholarly work]. *Le mouvement social, 63,* 109–124.

Perry, M. (1979). Literary dynamics: How the order of a text creates its meanings. *Poetics Today, 1*(1), 35–64.

Polletta, F., & Kai Ho, M. (2006). Frames and their consequences. In R. E. Goodin & C. Tilly (Eds.), *The Oxford handbook of contextual political analysis* (pp. 187–209). Oxford, UK: Oxford University Press.

Popping, R. (2000). *Computer-assisted text analysis.* Thousand Oaks, CA: Sage.

Poulantzas, N. (1970). *Fascism and dictatorship.* London: Verso.

Prince, G. (1973). *A grammar of stories: An introduction.* De Proprietatibus Litterarum Minor Series No. 13. The Hague: Mouton.

Propp, V. (1958). *Morphology of the folktale* (S. Pirkova-Jakobson, Ed.; L. Scott, Trans.). Bloomington: Indiana University Research Center in Anthropology, Folklore, and Linguistics. (Original work published 1928)

Propp, V. (1968). *Morphology of the folktale.* Austin: University of Texas Press. (Original work published 1928)

Ragin, C. C., & Rubinson, C. (2009). The distinctiveness of comparative research. In T. Landman & N. Robinson (Eds.), *The Sage handbook of comparative politics* (pp. 13–34). London: Sage.

Ragin, C. C. (1987). *The comparative method: Moving beyond qualitative and quantitative strategies.* Berkeley: University of California Press.

Ragin, C. C. (2000). *Fuzzy-set social science.* Chicago: University of Chicago Press.

Ragin, C. C. (2008). *Redesigning social inquiry: Fuzzy sets and beyond.* Chicago: University of Chicago Press.

Ramakrishnan, R., & Gehrke, J. (2002). *Database management systems.* New York: McGraw-Hill.

Reinharz, S. (1992). *Feminist methods in social research.* Oxford, UK: Oxford University Press.

Rickert, H. (1962). *Science and history: A critique of positivistic epistemology* (A. Goddard, Ed.). Princeton, NJ: D. Van Nostrand. (Original work published 1902)

Ricoeur, P. (1984). *Time and narrative* (K. McLaughlin & D. Pellauer, Trans.) (Vol. 1). Chicago: University of Chicago Press.

Ricoeur, P. (1985). *Time and narrative* (K. McLaughlin & D. Pellauer, Trans.) (Vol. 2). Chicago: University of Chicago Press.

Ricoeur, P. (1988). *Time and narrative* (K. McLaughlin & D. Pellauer, Trans.) (Vol. 3). Chicago: University of Chicago Press.

Rimmon-Kenan, S. (1983). *Narrative fiction: Contemporary poetics.* London: Methuen.

Roberts, C. W. (1989). Other than counting words: A linguistic approach to content analysis. *Social Forces, 68*(1), 147–177.

Roberts, C. W. (1997). A generic semantic grammar for quantitative text analysis: Applications to East and West Berlin radio news content from 1979. In A. Raftery (Ed.), *Sociological methodology* (Vol. 27, pp. 89–129). Oxford, UK: Basil Blackwell.

Roberts, R. H., & Good, J. M. M. (Eds.). (1993). *The recovery of rhetoric: Persuasive discourse and disciplinarity in the human sciences.* Charlottesville: University of Virginia Press.

Rosaldo, R. (1993). *Culture & truth: The remaking of social analysis. With a new introduction* (2nd ed.). Boston: Beacon Press. (Original work published 1989)

Rueschemeyer, D., Stephens, E. H., & Stephens, J. D. (1992). *Capitalist development and democracy.* Chicago: University of Chicago Press.

Rumelhart, D. (1975). Notes on a schema for stories. In D. Bobrow & A. Collins (Eds.), *Representation and understanding* (pp. 211–236). New York: Academic Press.

Schrodt, P. A. (2006). Twenty years of the Kansas event data system project. *The political methodologist, 14*(1), 2–6.

Skvoretz, J. (1993). Generating narratives from simple action structures. *Journal of Mathematical Sociology, 18*(2/3), 135–140.

Skvoretz, J., & T. J. Fararo. (1989). Action structures and sociological action theory. *Journal of Mathematical Sociology, 14*(2/3), 111–137.

Smith, T. (2007). Narrative boundaries and the dynamics of ethnic conflict and conciliation. *Poetics, 35,* 22–46.

Smitherman, G. (1994). *Black talk: Words and phrases from the hood to the amen corner.* Boston: Houghton Mifflin.

Snow, D. A., Rochford, R. B., Jr., Worden, S. K., & Benford, R. D. (1986). Frame alignment processes, micromobilization, and movement participation. *American Sociological Review, 51*(4), 464–481.

Snowden, F. M. (1986). *Violence and the great estates in the South of Italy: Apulia, 1900–1922.* Cambridge, UK: Cambridge University Press.

Snowden, F. M. (1989). *The fascist revolution in Tuscany, 1919–1922.* Cambridge, UK: Cambridge University Press.

Stein, N. L. (1982a). The definition of a story. *Journal of Pragmatics, 6,* 487–507.

Stein, N. L. (1982b). What's in a story: Interpreting the interpretations of story grammars. *Discourse Processes, 5*(3/4), 319–335.

Stein, N. L., & Glenn, C. G. (1979). An analysis of story comprehension in elementary school children. In R. Freedle (Ed.), *New directions in discourse processing* (pp. 53–120). Norwood, NJ: Ablex.

Stein, N. L., & Policastro, M. (1984). The concept of a story: A comparison between children's and teacher's perspectives. In H. Mandl, N. L. Stein, & T. Trabasso (Eds.), *Learning and comprehension of text* (pp. 113–55). Hillsdale, NJ: Lawrence Erlbaum.

Steinberg, S. J., & Steinberg, S. L. (2006). *Geographic information systems for the social sciences.* Thousand Oaks: Sage.

Stone, P. J., Dunphy, D. C., Smith, M. S., & Ogilvie, D. M. (1966). *The general inquirer: A computer approach to content analysis.* Cambridge, MA: MIT Press.

Tannen, D. (1994). *Gender and discourse.* New York: Oxford University Press.

Taylor, J. (2004). *Linguistic categorization* (3rd ed.). Oxford, UK: Oxford University Press.

Taylor, S. J., & Bogdan, R. (1984). *Introduction to qualitative research methods: The search for meaning.* New York: Wiley.

Thomas, W. I., & Znaniecki, F. (1918). *The Polish peasant in Europe and America. Monograph of an immigrant group: Vol. 2. Primary-group organization.* Boston: Richard G. Badger/Gorham Press.

Tilly, C. (1995). *Popular contention in Great Britain, 1758–1834.* Cambridge, MA: Harvard University Press.

Tilly, C. (2008). *Credit and blame.* Princeton, NJ: Princeton University Press.

Tilly, C., Tilly, L., & Tilly, R. (1975). *The rebellious century, 1830–1930.* Cambridge, MA: Harvard University Press.

Todorov, T. (1969). *Grammaire du* Décaméron [The grammar of the *Decameron*]. The Hague: Mouton.

Todorov, T. (1977). *The poetics of prose* (R. Howard, Trans.). Oxford, UK: Basil Blackwell. (Original work published 1971)

Todorov, T. (1981). *Introduction to poetics* (R. Howard, Trans.). Sussex, UK: Harvester Press. (Original work published 1968)

Todorov, T. (1990). *Genres in discourse.* Cambridge, UK: Cambridge University Press. (Original work published 1978)

162

Tomashevski, B. (1965). Thematics. In L. Lemon & M. Reis (Eds.). *Russian formalist criticism: Four essays* (pp. 61–95). Lincoln: University of Nebraska Press. (Original work published 1925)

Toolan, M. (1988). *Narrative: A critical linguistic introduction.* London: Routledge.

Toynbee, A. J. (1946). *A study of history* (Abridgement of Vols. I–VI by D. C. Somervell). Oxford, UK: Oxford University Press.

Trew, A. (1979a). Theory and ideology at work. In R. Fowler, R. Hodge, G. Kress, & A. Trew (Eds.), *Language and control* (pp. 94–116). London: Routledge & Kegan Paul.

Trew, A. (1979b). What the papers say: Linguistic variation and ideological difference. In R. Fowler, R. Hodge, G. Kress, & A. Trew (Eds.), *Language and control* (pp. 117–156). London: Routledge & Kegan Paul.

Tuchman, G. (1972). Objectivity as a strategic ritual. *American Journal of Sociology, 77,* 660–679.

Tully, J. (Ed.). (1988). *Meaning and context: Quentin Skinner and his critics.* Princeton, NJ: Princeton University Press.

van Dijk, T. (1972). *Some aspects of text grammars.* The Hague: Mouton.

van Dijk, T. (1980). Story comprehension: An introduction. *Poetics, 9,* 1–21.

van Dijk, T. (1983). Discourse analysis: Its development and application to the structure of news. *Journal of Communication, 33*(2), 20–43.

van Dijk, T. (1988). *News as discourse.* Hillsdale, NJ: Lawrence Erlbaum.

van Dijk, T. (Ed.). (1985). *Handbook of discourse analysis* (Vols. 1–4). London: Academic Press.

Van Maanen, J. (1988). *Tales of the Field. On Writing Ethnography.* Chicago: University of Chicago Press.

Vicari, S. (2008). *Contemporary protest: The online framing of local and global dynamics* (Doctoral dissertation, University of Reading, UK, 2008).

Vickers, B. (1988). *In defence of rhetoric.* Oxford, UK: Clarendon Press.

Wasserman, S., & Faust, K. (1994). *Social network analysis in the social and behavioral sciences.* Cambridge, UK: Cambridge University Press.

Wada, T. (2004). Event analysis of claim making in Mexico: How are social protests transformed into political protests? *Mobilization: An International Journal, 9*(3), 241–257.

Weber, M. (1978). *Economy and society. An outline of interpretive sociology.* Berkeley: University of California Press. (Original work published 1922)

Weber, R. P. (1990). *Basic content analysis.* Newbury Park, CA: Sage.

Windelband, W. (1980). History and natural science. *History and Theory, 19*(2), 165–185. (Original work published 1894)

AUTHOR INDEX

166

Sikes, M. P., 39
Silver, C., 6, 59n 2, 63, 102n 1
Simon, H., 92
Skinner, Q., 17
Skvoretz, J., 41
Smelser, N., 141n 8
Smith, M. S., 103n 3
Smith, T., 43, 51
Smitherman, G., 146
Snow, D. A., 49
Snowden, F. M., 125
Statham, P., 43, 56n 17, 100, 153n 1
Stein, N. L., 98
Steinberg, S. J., 124
Steinberg, S. L., 124
Stephens, E. H., 77
Stephens, J. D., 77
Stone, P. J., 103n 3
Stovel, K., 42, 57n 31
Strauss, A. L., 60

Tannen, D., 146
Taylor, C. L., 62
Taylor, J., 92
Taylor, S. J., 38, 40, 57n 27
Thomas, W. I., 11
Tilly, C., 36, 43, 50, 76, 92, 148
Tilly, L., 76
Tilly, R., 76
Todorov, T., 2, 12, 13, 17, 20, 22, 23,
    55n 3, 55n 4, 55n 7, 55n 9, 56n 18

Tomashevski, 55n 7
Tomashevski, B., 13, 55n 3, 55n 7,
    55n 8
Toolan, M., 12, 13, 16, 17, 18, 22, 55n
    2, 55n 5, 56, 56n 20
Toynbee, A. J., 5
Trew, A., 146
Tuchman, G., 146
Tully, J., 56n 15

van Dijk, T., 18, 23, 24, 44, 45, 55,
    55n 10, 56, 56n 12, 56n 16, 57,
    57n 23
Van Maanen, J., 57 n28
Vicari, S., 6, 47, 48, 58n 38, 140
Vickers, B., 58n 40

Wada, T., 43, 110,
    141n 1, 150
Waletzky, J., 3, 10n 2, 14, 16,
    55n 2, 56n 12
Wasserman, S., 110
Watts, D., 141n 3
Weber, M., 132
Weber, R. P., 3
Weitman, S., 35
Windelband, W., 104n 11
Worden, S. K., 49

Znaniecki, F., 11
Zuell, C., 102n 1

SUBJECT INDEX

Note: In page references, f indicates figures and t indicates tables.

167

173

Supporting researchers for more than 40 years

Research methods have always been at the core of SAGE's publishing program. Founder Sara Miller McCune published SAGE's first methods book, *Public Policy Evaluation*, in 1970. Soon after, she launched the *Quantitative Applications in the Social Sciences* series—affectionately known as the "little green books."

Always at the forefront of developing and supporting new approaches in methods, SAGE published early groundbreaking texts and journals in the fields of qualitative methods and evaluation.

Today, more than 40 years and two million little green books later, SAGE continues to push the boundaries with a growing list of more than 1,200 research methods books, journals, and reference works across the social, behavioral, and health sciences. Its imprints—Pine Forge Press, home of innovative textbooks in sociology, and Corwin, publisher of PreK–12 resources for teachers and administrators—broaden SAGE's range of offerings in methods. SAGE further extended its impact in 2008 when it acquired CQ Press and its best-selling and highly respected political science research methods list.

From qualitative, quantitative, and mixed methods to evaluation, SAGE is the essential resource for academics and practitioners looking for the latest methods by leading scholars.

For more information, visit **www.sagepub.com**.